Bill Gentile's
Essential
Video Journalism
Field Manual

By Backpack Journalist Bill Gentile

Second Edition

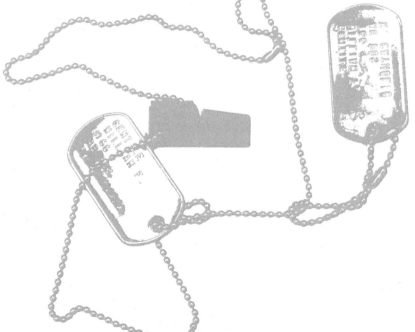

BillGentile.com

Bill Gentile's Essential Video Journalism Field Manual
By Bill Gentile
© Copyright Bill Gentile 2016

Second Edition for North America
Published by The Backpack Journalist, LLC

Front Cover Photo by Bill Gentile
Betsy Dufault, Assistant Editor
Esther Gentile, Assistant Editor
Matt Morris, Assistant Editor, Second Edition
Daniela Pérez Frías, Assistant Editor

For information please contact
Bill Gentile
billgentile@billgentile.com • (202) 492-6405

Book designed and produced by J. Bruce Jones, Bruce Jones Design Inc.

I dedicate this work to my mother, Maria Theresa D'Eramo, and to my father, Guerino Frank Gentile. They made everything possible.

– Bill Gentile
July 2016

Acknowledgements

To the people whose grace and generosity of spirit have allowed me to tell their stories, I extend my deepest appreciation. To my brothers, other members of my Family and loved ones who have given me the patience and unconditional support through good times and bad, I thank you. To my wife, Esther, who has been at my side on this long journey.

Table of Contents

Before We Begin

Welcome to the second edition of my Essential Video Journalism Field Manual.

This manual is the distillation of 40 years of work in the field as a visual communicator. Drawing from a deep well of personal, real-life experiences across disciplines and from some of the farthest and most challenging corners of the globe, I bring to you the tools of powerful visual communication. Read this manual and learn to make compelling films!

Who should read this manual? This manual is for beginning filmmakers, documentarians and visual storytellers, for those with some experience, and for those more seasoned practitioners who want to sharpen their skills and acquire new ones. Print journalists seeking to expand their skills will discover in these pages a dynamic new world of communication. Broadcast journalists accustomed to the technology and techniques preceding today's hand-held digital cameras will find that today's equipment delivers a more immediate, more intimate version of visual communication than did their predecessors. Still photojournalists making the transition to film and video will find the manual instructive, despite their already-existing understanding of composition, of light vs. darkness, of motion, etc. They will discover that those skills alone do not make a video journalist.

Quick story: By the late 1980s and early 1990s, I saw the writing on the wall. And that writing said, "The craft of photojournalism is contracting, and the craft of video journalism is expanding." Partly because of what I saw happening to our craft, I left my post at Newsweek magazine. (And this is when I was working as a contract photographer for Newsweek, which was one of the most coveted jobs in the profession.) And I began working for Video News International (VNI), the first company in the United States to use the new, hand-held, consumer cameras hitting the market, to produce content for television. (More on this later.)

VNI spent millions of dollars training professional journalists to become video journalists, or "VJs," as we called ourselves. But only a handful of us, including myself, became true video journalists capable of producing television content as a one-person team. Why was I one of the very few VNI trainees to become a VJ? Because by the time I made the transition to video, I already had worked as a reporter, editor, and photojournalist for a daily newspaper; as a photojournalist, foreign correspondent and editor for United Press International (UPI); as a "stringer" radio correspondent for ABC News and for NBC News. In other words, I already had acquired the skills of picture-making, writing, editing and narrating that are so critical to the craft of video journalism.

So although pictures are the engine that drive this methodology, it takes more than just pretty pictures to tell powerful visual stories. This manual explains how we employ all these skills to make stories. There is something in this manual for everyone. My hope is that you will find that "something," and you will use it to enhance your craft, your life and the lives of those around you.

OK. Let's begin.

Introduction: A Ticket and a Tool

It was July 20, 1979 and I sat on the rooftop balcony of the Intercontinental Hotel overlooking what was left of Managua, Nicaragua. The Sandinista insurrection had just ended, leaving more than 30,000 dead, and a nation of 3.5 million was free of a U.S.-backed dictatorship that had ruled for decades. I was a "stringer" for United Press International (UPI), covering as photojournalist and correspondent the first of what would be a series of conflicts, mostly in Latin America but as far away as Africa, Iraq and Afghanistan.

This was a new world. It was the first time I had seen combat, violence used to achieve political ends, refugees, and dead bodies in the street. My new world was peopled with smart, sophisticated journalists, corrupt politicians, mean, violent soldiers, spooks from intelligence services around the world, foreign fighters, real and wannabe revolutionaries, hangers-on, winners and losers.

I was working mostly as a photographer then, going out every day with pockets full of raw, black-and-white Kodak Tri-X film, hoping to bring them back filled with compelling, prize-winning images of the war. I returned every day and handed the film over to Lou Garcia, at that time UPI's regional photo editor, the quintessential photojournalist, mentor and guy who could get in, get the pictures, and get out.

Lou would develop my film in the darkroom he hauled from story to story, setting it up in hotel bathrooms and locking out light with sheets of black plastic and gaffer's tape. He developed the film, made the 8X10 inch prints, wrote the captions and then sat up half the night transmitting the prints over telephone lines to UPI headquarters in New York

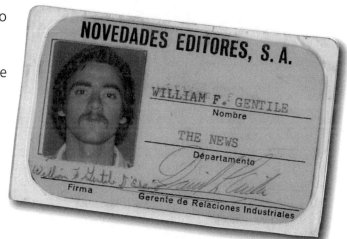

My transition from print media to backpack video journalism began here, as reporter/editor/photographer at the English-language Mexico City NEWS, a sister publication of the larger Novedades Editores, S.A. I landed a 10-week internship at the paper right out of graduate school. I stayed at the paper for a year, until I started to work as a stringer foreign correspondent for United Press International (UPI) in Mexico City.

where they would be directed to clients all over the world. It took 14 minutes to transmit a single black-and-white photograph from Managua, Nicaragua, to New York.

I was light years away from the small steel town of Aliquippa, Pennsylvania, just outside of Pittsburgh, where I had grown up. Aliquippa was where my grandfathers arrived from Italy to work in the steel mills, where all my uncles had worked, where my father had worked, where my three brothers and I all had worked, though for brief periods.

The mill was a place where men toiled in eight-hour shifts 24-hours a day, all year round. The mill never stopped. Men worked near blast furnaces that baked them from 50 yards away. They climbed over and around stacks of steel that weighed thousands of pounds each and with one mistake could topple over and crush them like paper cups. They froze in the winter and cooked in the summer.

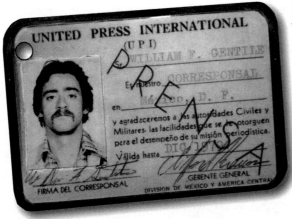

I knew there was something beyond this place and I knew I wanted to find it. Though my parents were Italian immigrants with little formal education, they had the wisdom to bring the world into our home, mostly through newspapers and magazines. I think the seed of my need to explore came in the form of Life magazine and its stunning pictures of the Vietnam War.

Somehow I had figured out that journalism could be a **ticket and a tool**, both of which I yearned for. A ticket in the sense that it could deliver me from a life in the steel mills where I was certain I never wanted to return after working my way through college; and a tool in that it would allow me to engage in, and hopefully impact, the world around me, like the pictures from Vietnam had made an impact on me.

I became a journalist, heading right out of graduate school to Mexico City to work as reporter/photographer/editor for the English-language, Mexico City News. Eventually I would teach the craft of journalism.

To this day, in my "Photojournalism and Social Documentary" class at American University, I use the work of Life magazine's famed photojournalist Larry Burrows to exemplify the power of still photojournalism. Curiously, the methodology that today we refer to as "video journalism," or "backpack video journalism," is built upon the shoulders of documentary-style photojournalism practiced by the men and women who covered that conflict.

This image by Larry Burrows of Life magazine is one of the many pictures of the war in Vietnam that made a deep impression on me and impacted my decision to pursue a career in journalism.

As I sat on that balcony of the Intercontinental Hotel in Managua, I knew I had confirmed my sense that journalism was my ticket out of the drudgery of the steel mills and the routine of domestic life.

Eventually, I also came to understand that journalism can be a tool. What I wrote years later on the home page of my Web site (www.billgentile.com) summarizes how I feel about the craft today:

> I began my career in the golden days of journalism when the craft still was about information as opposed to entertainment, and when the men and women who practiced the craft believed that information can make a difference. That belief has often taken me to places inhabited by the poor, the illiterate and the oppressed, places where journalists are so desperately needed. In all of these places, I have found people with the grace, the dignity and the generosity of spirit to allow me to tell their stories, to practice my craft. The work that you see here exists largely because the people depicted allowed me to work among them. I am deeply grateful for that privilege, and this work is a tribute to them. I hope it has made a difference.

EDITORS: THIS IS A RECROPPED VERSION OF NIP062305
NIP062308-6/23/79-MANAGUA: Shaking with terror, a woman pleads with a Nicaraguan National
Guard trooper to permit her to reenter her home in the Don Bosco barrio of Managua to
bring out her husband and son after the area had been pounded by heavy artillery and roc-
kets early 6/23. UPI /1968907 lg/William Gentile

As you read this now, more than ever, the tools we have at our fingertips are more powerful than any in history. In June of 2009 I gave a presentation on "backpack video journalism" at the Harvard Club in New York City. Here's part of what I said:

> *"We are, right now, at an extraordinary juncture in the history of mankind, technology and communication. Even more important than the Gutenberg press, the advances in digital cameras and the Internet provide us unprecedented opportunity. Ordinary citizens of the world now wield extraordinary power. We wield the power to communicate instantly, globally and in a language, the visual language, which supersedes both the written and the spoken word. This visual language knows no frontiers. It needs no translation. It is contingent on no corporate support. It is one of the most powerful tools of our time…And backpack journalism is the embodiment of this visual language."*

We wield power that Lou Garcia and I couldn't even imagine back when we covered the insurrection in Nicaragua. I write this book in 2012. Technology has rocketed me such a long way from Aliquippa, Pennsylvania, to Managua, Nicaragua, and finally to Washington, DC, where I live today. The craft has introduced me to places and people that I never would have known had I not chosen this path. It's time now for me to pass along some of my experiences and lessons to you. I want you to benefit from my experiences and make the difference that YOU want to make.

So come with me on this new journey, as I explain the keys to the methodology that we refer to as "backpack video journalism." I'll teach you how to use the ticket and the tool that I've used for the past four decades. Your job is to embrace my lessons and to make a difference.

This book is laid out in the approximate fashion and order of my Video Journalism Workshops. Having said that, I tailor each workshop to the specifics of each group. Some are large and some small. Some are more advanced than others. Some need more focus on production and others on post-production.

These are two of my images transmitted from Managua, Nicaragua, to United Press International (UPI) headquarters in New York City during the 1979 Sandinista Revolution in Nicaragua. After developing the film, printing the image, writing the caption on a manual typewriter – all in a makeshift hotel darkroom – it took 14 minutes over a long-distance telephone line to transmit each image to New York.

I.
Pre-Production

Pre-Production: The preparatory stage of video journalism, or backpack video journalism. This stage includes everything you need to do before picking up your gear and heading to the field.

By the mid-1980s, I had left UPI and signed on as Newsweek Magazine's Contract Photographer for Latin America and the Caribbean. I was based in Managua, Nicaragua, and my territory included everything from the Rio Grande to the tip of South America, as well as the entire Caribbean, including Haiti and Cuba. By this time I no longer was using black-and-white film and telephone-based transmission. Instead, I was using color slides and shipping the raw film from the field to Newsweek's headquarters in New York.

As a measure of how technology has affected our craft, shortly before this writing, Newsweek announced that it no longer would be a hard copy (paper) publication, but an online version of its previous self.

Definition

So let's define "backpack journalism," or "backpack video journalism" before we move on. It's critical that we understand exactly what this thing is, and what it is not.

From my blog, I define the craft as:

> Backpack journalism is the craft of one **properly trained practitioner** using a **hand-held digital video camera** to tell **character-driven** stories in a more **immediate, more intimate** fashion than is achievable using a conventional, shoulder-held camera and a team that includes camera person, sound person, correspondent and producer. Backpack journalists do it all and, most importantly, we make the pictures, which are the driving force of visual communication. (There's a reason they call it tele-VISION.) In the field, a backpack journalist shoots, acquires sound, produces, reports, interviews. We write the script. In some cases we narrate the piece. Depending on circumstances, we either edit the piece on our own, or we sit side-by-side with an editor assigned to the task.
>
> Backpack journalism is not the 6 o'clock news reported by a single, multi-tasking journalist. It is a character-driven methodology with a specific, **time-consuming** approach and application that yields unique results and that **does not work in all situations**.

Some clarification here. I sometimes use the terms "video journalism," "backpack journalism" and "backpack video journalism" interchangeably. The term "video journalism" first was used by **Video News International (VNI),** the first company in the United States (and I suspect the world) to use the emerging, mini-DV consumer cameras to generate television programming. I went to work for them in 1995 at their base in Philadelphia, PA. Michael Rosenblum founded the company. Today Michael calls himself "The Father of Video Journalism." And he has good reason to do so, because he was way before his time in recognizing the profound changes initiated by the **revolution in technology.** We called the practitioners of the craft "VJs." You may have seen some of our early work on "The Learning Channel." We were the people who produced, "Trauma: Life in the ER," which for a long time was the most popular series broadcast by that outlet. I shot a ton of these shows for them. In fact, I shot a significant part of the pilot show, which we did at a hospital right there in Philadelphia. (Sadly the company failed and eventually was absorbed to become The New York Times Television Company, but that's another story.)

I consider myself a pioneer in what I call "backpack journalism," which is an "edgier" version of video journalism. One of my colleagues calls it, "**run & gun,**" in comparison with the more civilized or sedate "video journalism" version of the craft.

In 2007 I introduced the term, "backpack journalism" at the **American University (AU) School of Communication in Washington, DC,** where I still teach at this writing. I adapted an existing course at AU and introduced the backpack methodology. In the fall of the same year I hosted a seminar called, "Photojournalism: Surviving the Digital Challenge." In May of 2008 I embedded with the 24th Marine Expeditionary Unit (24th MEU) in a major offensive in the Helmand River Valley in Afghanistan. During that three-week assignment for NOW on PBS, I carried everything I needed to do my job in my backpack: camera, computer, external hard drives, batteries, shotgun and wireless microphones, toiletries, clothes. The works. I wore a heavy bullet-proof vest and helmet. Like the Marines I was covering, on patrol I carried my own food and water – in 120-degree heat. My story was nominated for a national Emmy Award. Called, "**Afghanistan: The Forgotten War,**" it lost out to Anderson Cooper and his two-part series on rape in the Congo. I'm proud to have competed in the same arena as his outfit and some of the other competitors, all major U.S. television outlets using the older, muscle-bound model of television production. This trip is where and when the term "backpack" really made sense to me. In December of that same year I conducted the first Backpack Journalism Workshop With NOW on PBS at the American Film Institute (AFI) in Silver Spring, MD. In March of 2010 I launched the **Backpack Journalism Project at American University.**

Week of 10.2.09
Afghanistan: The Forgotten War

On the front lines with Marines in Afghanistan: Can we defeat a resurgent Taliban?

NOW on PBS Correspondent Bill Gentile reports from Afghanistan's southern Helmand Province, where he was embedded for nearly three weeks in the summer of 2008 with the 24th Marine Expeditionary Unit (24th MEU).

In 2008 I traveled to Afghanistan to embed with the 24th Marine Expeditionary Unit (24thMEU) as it conducted a major offensive in the Helmand River Valley on the border with Pakistan. The piece was a finalist in the national Emmy Award competition, losing out to Anderson Cooper's two-part series on rape in the Congo.

Prior to launching American University's Backpack Journalism Project, our School of Communication commissioned a research paper on the subject. Below is an excerpt from an early version of that paper, which is written by Tom Kennedy. I think it raises some key issues:

> *Backpack Journalism is an alternative approach to journalistic story-telling that fuses audio and video reporting, with one person functioning to do the reporting, photography, narration, production and editing tasks to create a finished product.*

> *It is a method using visual journalism to create powerful, intimate stories that take people beyond the boundary of their own life experience and connect them with the currents, forces, and situations reshaping our world on a daily basis. Using multiple media tools, backpack journalists create content that engages* **audience intellect and emotion** *simultaneously.*

> *The fruits of the approach occur because a journalist is being given the* **tools, time, and freedom to assume the responsibilities of personal authorship** *to craft a story with value to an audience. Personal authorship is rooted in intimate connection with the story's subjects. That in turn permits extended periods of observation that get to the heart of a story.*

> *Because of changes in the technology used to create journalism, changes in methods of content delivery to the audience, and economic pressures to streamline news gathering costs, backpack journalism has arrived as an alternative process for creating* **documentary-style narrative journalism**.

The technology available today allows us to practice this new methodology that we refer to as video journalism, or backpack video journalism. It has democratized the craft. No longer do we have to work for giant media conglomerates to participate in the international exchange of information. You and I have a place at the table in this conversation. But first we have to know how to speak the language. This manual will instruct you on how to do exactly that.

From the above definitions, these are the words and phrases that you should remember:

- **Properly-trained.**
- **Character-driven.**
- **Intimate and immediate.**
- **Time-consuming.**
- **Does not work in all situations.**
- **Audience intellect and emotion.**
- **Tools, time and freedom.**
- **Personal authorship.**
- **Documentary-style narrative journalism.**

The foundation of backpack video journalism is **documentary-style photojournalism**. It's the kind of stuff that Newsweek Magazine allowed me to do during the 1980s as I tromped through the mountains and the mean streets of Central America, spending weeks and sometimes a month at a time with protagonists in the region, getting to know them, getting to the heart of the story – very much unlike the wire service or TV guys who were restricted to the mandates of the clock, the calendar and the bean counters, and were given limited time to acquire the information needed to tell their stories.

That's what this field manual is about. Backpack video journalism.

What you should expect

This field manual, the Backpack Documentary classes that I teach at American University, as well as the **Video Journalism Workshops** that I conduct outside of the university, all are broken up into three parts, pretty much like the process of documentary making or video storytelling in real life. We go through the **pre-production** phase, which is coming up with story ideas and writing a proposal for that story idea, pitching the story idea, and doing the preliminary investigation to figure out everything you can before actually heading to the field to start the production phase.

The **production** phase is the second part in which you actually pull out the camera and hit the ground and start to shoot, finding and defining characters, cultivating those characters and their dramatic arcs, and getting to the heart of the story through them.

The third phase is when you get back to your home or office or the editing suite and sit in front of the computer and actually put the piece together. We call this **post-production**.

My job here is to download as accessibly as I can, as efficiently as I can, my 40 years in the field practicing the craft of visual communication. My job is to articulate the lessons learned as a correspondent and photojournalist for United Press International (UPI), as Newsweek Magazine's Contract Photographer for Latin America and the Caribbean, as backpack video journalist for Video News International (VNI), The New York Times Television Company, The Learning Channel, the Discovery Channel, National Geographic Television, ABC's Nightline With Ted Koppel, NOW With Bill Moyers, NOW hosted by David Brancaccio, Court TV and Lion TV, and as an independent documentary filmmaker for a number of outlets, domestic and foreign.

A note on **"citizen journalism"**

We all are familiar with this term. It typically is used to describe the practice by citizens, not normally considered professional journalists, who collect, process and distribute information, largely over social media. This work can be extremely valuable in documenting violations of human rights, for example, or in situations or countries where the practice of professional journalism is restricted. As in other forms of visual communication, many of the principles I cover in this manual are applicable in citizen journalism, as well.

A New Language

This field manual, my classes and my workshops all are about a new language. The **visual language.** This language has its own alphabet, its own ABCs and new words like close-ups, medium shots, wide-angle shots. They all are basic components of this new language.

As you work on your video story you should be keeping a mental list of the different kinds of shots that you have at your disposal. You should use these different kinds of shots to build the elements of your story. The key here is to make videos that move, and you can't just be shooting wide-angle after wide-angle after wide-angle because it becomes visually repetitive and very boring. Your task is to tell visual stories that are compelling and interesting. The engine inside the video journalism methodology is imagery that tells a compelling story. If you don't tell a story with compelling images that move, then your story just won't be very interesting.

The current revolution in technology is a double-edged sword. On one hand this technology now is accessible to a vast portion of citizens around the world who can use it for making positive changes in the world. On the other hand this technology now is accessible to a vast portion of citizens around the world who can use it for making positive changes in the world. Get it? The fact that everybody and her brother has access to this technology doesn't mean that people know how to use it. On the contrary, most people don't, and this is evidenced by looking at the mush we see on television and the Internet. It's called "**spray and pray.**" In other words, put a wide-angle lens on the camera, blast everything in sight and then pray that something comes out that's useable. This is not an appropriate use of the technology or the opportunity presented by this technology. It's not a proper use of the visual language. It does not reflect an understanding or literacy of that language.

Take a look at the evening news. Images are treated as second-class citizens. They are used as wallpaper behind the editorial line presented by the anchor or the correspondent, or as filler between talking heads. It's a missed opportunity.

The methodology that we refer to as "video journalism" or "backpack video journalism" is composed of **three components: images, natural sound and narration**. Images are the driving force of the medium. Images are the engine inside this medium. Nothing moves without them. Why, then, would you reduce images to second-class citizenry as wallpaper behind the anchor or correspondent, or as filler between talking heads?

In the best documentaries, you should be able to kill the sound and follow the story by just looking at the images. I make visual stories. I build visual stories. I shoot visual stories. And when I get to the editing suite, I select natural sound, or audio, from characters that build upon, or strengthen, those visual stories. And I **write narration TO the pictures**. I write the narration to build upon those visual stories. This is a profoundly different approach to storytelling. This is video journalism.

What we do **NOT** do is illustrate print stories.

In 2005 I traveled alone to Afghanistan to make a film about foreign correspondents, called, "FRONTLINE JOURNALISTS: Death and Danger in Afghanistan." So I followed a number of foreign correspondents while they did their job. Afghanistan is one of the most visually compelling countries in the world, so making powerful images outside was not a problem.

However, I had to be creative to make strong images inside the news bureaus of the correspondents I followed around. And I did so by looking for special angles, like this second shot of BBC Correspondent Andrew North while he's writing a story . . .

...or this silhouette of New York Times Correspondent Carlotta Gall.

If this methodology uses **images as the engine** or driving force, it uses character to make the emotional and intellectual connection. Remember, the best stories are told through the prism of **one person's experience.** It can be one person, one football team, one high school class, one professor, one platoon. Think of Oliver Stone's movie, "Platoon," in which he used a single military unit to tell the story of the entire Vietnam experience.

We'll discuss **character and the selection of character** later but you should keep this in mind as we progress.

When I'm in the field I'm building a visual story in my mind. The first step of this process is to **de-construct the story** that's in front of you. Once you de-construct it you can **document it**. Then you can **RE-construct** it when you get back to the editing suite.

I'm thinking about what we see first, what we see last, and what we see in the middle of a visual story. I'm laying the story out, on the timeline in my mind. I carry a **reporter's notebook** with me, as well. And I'm writing the script and the treatment as I shoot the story. I also use the reporter's notebook to begin writing narration.

Having said that, **my primary reporting tool is the camera**. Out of the camera I get the video and the audio for my documentary or video story. I also get ambient sound and people's voices for radio. I can pull screen shots from the high-definition images that I make with the video camera. From the interviews, I get background information and quotes for print stories. This is where technology has taken us today.

There was a time when we journalists couldn't imagine the possibilities that technology could offer. And such control. When I first started out as a journalist in Mexico City, we used separate tools for each separate task. Manual typewriters for print journalists. Heavy, clunky cameras and lenses for photographers. Cumbersome recorders for radio correspondents. And TV? Forget about it. TV crews consisted of a cameraman (they were mostly men big and strong enough to carry around heavy, shoulder-held cameras) a sound man hooked by hard wire to the camera (also mostly men), a producer (some women there) and a correspondent (mostly men). And the people behind the camera were not really journalists. The cameras were so complex that the camera person had to be a technician, not a journalist.

Now, if you know how to use the cameras of today properly, you can do all of these things by yourself. And you'll see the difference between this methodology as opposed to "spray and pray."

So how is our methodology different from what we normally see? It uses visuals as the driving force. It's a visual medium. By not having the correspondent inserted between the audience and the subjects, we have a more intimate and more immediate way of telling stories. Video journalism is a methodology that employs a single person to tell a much more intimate, more immediate story than is achievable using a large camera with a multi-person crew. **These small cameras offer extraordinary advantages.** They actually give subjects a sense that they have some control over the creative process. Subjects are not afraid of the camera. In fact, the camera actually engages them. It empowers them.

I learned this on a trip to Africa with my colleague and friend, Joanne Levine. Still working with VNI, we pitched two pieces to ABC's Nightline With Ted Koppel. One was about the systematic rape conducted by Hutu militias of women belonging to the rival Tutsi ethnic group in Rwanda during the 1994 genocide. We intended to interview rape victims – some of them forced to service dozens of Hutu men for weeks at a time during the 100-day genocide in which some 800,000 Tutsis and moderate Hutus were slaughtered.

Some of our colleagues at the home base in Philadelphia thought we were crazy. They asked: So, two white Westerners, one of them a male, are going to Rwanda to interview women who were savagely, repeatedly raped during the genocide, right? And these women are going to open right up to you and talk about it, is that correct?

"Yes," we said. "That's correct."

And that's exactly what happened. Not only did the women speak with us on camera. They poured their hearts out. They <u>wanted</u> to speak with us – because nobody else would. They had become pariahs in their own society. They were blamed for somehow being complicit in their own violation. Our encounters with them were catharsis. It was healing. It was heartbreaking.

There's an interesting side story here. Prior to our visit to Rwanda, rape had never been prosecuted as a "war crime." Rape always had been considered an incidental crime to the act of killing. Our story won the Robert F. Kennedy Award for Human Rights Reporting, Honorable Mention. After the story aired, Joanne had it sent to the International Tribunal at The Hague. Shortly afterward, rape began to be prosecuted as a war crime. Our story helped change international law. Pretty good for a couple of video journalists with a consumer camera, eh?

So it's very much the camera that makes this methodology possible. But you have to understand how the camera works. It has to be second nature when you head out into the field. You have to understand how to make the machine do on tape, or on a computer chip, what you see in your mind's eye. You can paint with these cameras. You can create with them. But you first have to know how to use them. (More on that later.)

These are screen shots I've pulled from the video I shot in Rwanda for a story on rape during the 1994 genocide. At top left are some of the bodies of Tutsis slaughtered during the killing that claimed an estimated 800,000 victims in 100 days. These people were killed in a school house where they had taken refuge then dumped in a common grave. After the genocide, the new Rwandan government recovered the bodies and placed them back in the school where they were killed. Today the school is a monument and a reminder. The other images show Tutsi women raped by Hutu militiamen during the genocide. These women opened up to my colleague and I in part because few of their own countrymen wanted to hear what they had to say. The women had been ostracized by Rwandan society for allegedly having been complicit in their own rape.

What Does Video Journalism Look Like?

The Limestone Correctional Facility in Alabama in the mid-1990s re-initiated the old practice of chaining together inmates working outside the prison facility. Officially, it was a very public way "to be tough on crime." Unofficially, it was a way for the prison system to save money. You need fewer guards to oversee prisoners chained together five at a time. When the story appeared on the front page of The New York Times every journalist in the world, or at least it seemed, showed up at the prison to do the story. The American wire services, major newspapers, television and radio outlets. The BBC and other foreign outlets sent crews. All were allowed to shoot the prisoners from the highway, which is public property. Some interviewed prison officials. But nobody got into the building that actually housed the chain gang.

I got to the Limestone Correction Facility in Alabama about a month after the new chain gang program was re-introduced. I think the warden granted me total access to the place because I was just one guy with a camera that looked like a toy, as opposed to a team of people with a pile of gear who might disrupt the place.

I visited the prison weeks after the story broke. It was the first assignment I took on for VNI. We called it, simply, "**Chain Gang**."

When I got to the prison the guy in charge asked me, "Where's the crew?"

I said, "I'm the crew."

He said, "Yeah, but where's the rest of the crew?"

"I'm all the crew there is," I said. "I'm it," explaining that I was cameraman, sound man, producer, fixer, correspondent.

"Oh," he said. Then he gave me total access to the place, telling me only to advise the appropriate officers when I left the prison, so I wouldn't get lost in the shuffle.

So for the next four days (all the time VNI allotted me) I arrived at the prison before sunup and left after sundown, shooting video in the prison yard, in the cafeteria, in the bunk area, even in the shower room. I had total, unfettered access.

I burned up over 20 hours of tape. (We were using mini-DV at the time.)

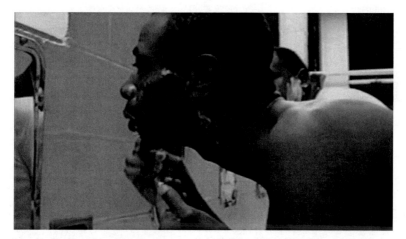

Largely because I was just one person with a hand-held camera, I was given total access to the Limestone Correctional Facility in Alabama. I even got to the shower area.

My editors at VNI loved it. They slammed together a 15-minute piece that they used to promote the company. They used it as a training video for new employees. To this day, some of the people who worked at VNI still use "Chain Gang" to define what video journalism looks like. Or, at least, should look like.

So what are the defining characteristics of "Chain Gang," and, by extension, what are the defining characteristics of powerful video journalism? Why is "Chain Gang" so good? Here's why:

• **Character.** I found two characters that looked, acted and sounded like they came straight out of Hollywood Central Casting. They passed my **three-point test of character:**

   (1) They wanted to be in the film.

   (2) They had great stories to tell.

   (3) They were incredibly articulate. (More about character selection later.)

I told the story of the chain gang through them. Their stories defied stereotypes.

• **Intimacy and immediacy.** I had no correspondent. No talking head. No filter between the story and the audience. There was nobody there interpreting the story for the audience. The story allowed the characters themselves to tell their own story as much as possible. I shot formal and informal interviews with prisoners, officers, the prison supervisor and warden. I shot what nearly turned out to be a riot by the inmates. Though you can occasionally hear my voice, there's never any confusion about who the protagonists are.

• **Strong visuals.** It is close-up and in your face. Take a look at some of the screen shots from video that I shot to tell the story. I built a powerful visual representation of the facility.

• **Length**. The piece is longer than what we typically see even on some of the best television magazine programs.

The main characters who emerged from a prison population of some 400 inmates passed my three-point test of character viability. (1) They wanted to be characters. (2) They had compelling stories to tell. (3) They were extremely articulate in telling them.

While at the facility I conducted informal and formal interviews; documented chains and weapons used to keep prisoners under control; and built a powerful visual representation of the facility.

Informal Interview

Formal Interview

Close-Up Chains

Wide Shot Officer With Rifle

Extra Wide Shot Prisoners

Multiple Planes

Close-Up Officer

Close-Up Officer

The ABCs of the Visual Language

Not just "Chain Gang" but every visual story you see or tell uses the same visual alphabet, or the ABCs of the visual language. Our written alphabet contains 26 letters. The visual alphabet contains about half that. We'll get to how we use the ABCs of the visual language during the production phase, but it's useful here to get a sense of what the alphabet looks like.

Please keep in mind that these definitions may differ somewhat from shop to shop, from outlet to outlet. Just like slang words can mean one thing in one part of the country and something different in another. But these are the fundamentals that are fairly standard across outlets. And we'll be using them throughout our relationship, so you should learn them and make them part of your new vocabulary.

Extra Close-Up (XCU)

Close-Up (CU)

Medium Shot (MS)

Extra Close-Up (XCU)

In the context of a face shot, the XCU would be just the eyes, or the glasses and the eyes.

Close-Up (CU)

The next shot is the CU, which is pretty much from the top of the head to the base of the chin. You can take off the top of the head, or the top of the hair, but you can never take off the chin, for two reasons. The first is that the audience wants to read the subject's mouth and expression, which are critical in deciphering whether a person is telling the truth or not. The second reason is that editors and producers might want to put the person's name under his/her face and you need the space at the bottom of the frame so as not to have lettering appear over the subject's mouth. We refer to this lettering as title or lower third.

Medium Shot (MS)

The MS runs from the top of the head to the waist or just below your belt. We need to see the belt.

Wide Shot (WS)

Extra Wide Shot (XWS)

Over the Shoulder (OTS)

Point of View (POV)

Wide Shot (WS)

The WS includes everything from your head to your toes.

Extra Wide Shot (XWS)

An XWS is even wider than a WS and might include visual information that's in front of and behind the subject. The XWS also are referred to as "Master" or "Establishing" shots because they show where all the elements in a scene are in relation to each other. You'll understand this better when we get to the Six-Shot System, which we'll go over shortly.

Over the Shoulder (OTS)

Shooting an OTS connects the subject with what he/she is doing. Especially in conjunction with other shots in the Six-Shot System, this shot is a particularly effective one in your toolbox of shots to make dynamic visual stories.

Point of View (POV)

The POV shows the viewer what the subject sees. For example, it's a shot of the keyboard that the typist is seeing. Or it's a shot of the road that the driver is seeing. Think of your subject coming through a door and walking through the room. You track the subject as he/she comes through the door and heads for the couch. Then, at a convenient time, you go back and come through the same door and walk the same path to the couch – with camera rolling as you do. That way the audience see's the subject's POV. The audience gets to see what the subject sees. This makes for a very dynamic view of what the subject sees when you can cut between these different kinds of shots.

The camera follows the subject across the scene.

Tracking Shot (Track)

In a Track, the camera follows the subject as the subject moves back and forth, or around a track (hence the name). Think of a camera following a race car around the track. The camera might also follow the subject coming into a room and moving over to the desk. That also would be a tracking shot. The cameraman stands still. The subject moves and the camera follows the subject.

In a pan, the subject doesn't move but the camera moves across the scene.

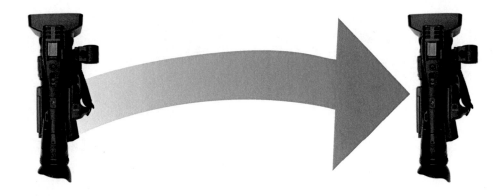

Pan Shot (Pan)

In a pan, the camera moves across the scene. Panning shots are really good if you want to illustrate an area such as a horizon, the front of the building or maybe a big crowd of people. Panning shots that move vertically or diagonally are often called "tilts."

When doing a pan or a tilt, it's important to do the reverse movement as well. Stated differently, if you pan left to right, make sure to pan back the other way. In the editing suite you'll be happy that you did, because this will give you the full range of material to work with. If you do a pan without a tripod, make sure that you are well braced on something like a table or a wall. Instead of just moving your arms, you want to make sure you use your whole body. This will give you stability. Also, make a decision about exactly where you want the pan to begin and where you want it to end. In other words, decide what you want to say with it. Another way to think of pans and tilts is that they act as "stitches" that connect pieces of visual material. They connect hands to a face, for example.

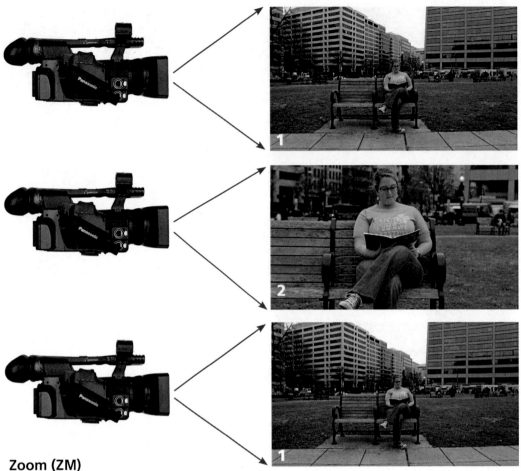

Zoom (ZM)

There are two kinds of zoom shots, one is executed with the camera and the other is done with your legs.

Camera starts with a extra wide shot, zooms into a wide shot, zooms back out to an extra wide shot.

Here's a quick list of the visual alphabet:

- **Extra Close-Up (XCU)**
- **Close-Up (CU)**
- **Medium Shot (MS)**
- **Wide Shot (WS)**
- **Extra Wide Shot (XWS)**

- **Tracking Shot (Track)**
- **Pan Shot (Pan)**
- **Zoom (ZM)**
- **Point of View (POV)**
- **Over the Shoulder (OTS)**

OK. Now we're all on the same page.

Story Ideas

So you want to tell visual stories. But how do you decide on a story idea? What makes a good visual story idea? Do all stories lend themselves to a visual telling? Which do? Which don't?

Take a look at the message that I send out to participants in my Video Journalism Workshops. I send it out weeks before the event begins. It should give you a good sense of what to look for in a potential visual story:

Hi All,

Your primary task during our Video Journalism Workshop is to conceive, produce, shoot, write, narrate and edit a 3-5 minute, character-driven documentary of your choice. At the end of the workshop, you will post your work on YouTube, Vimeo, or any online outlet that you prefer.

The first step is to come up with a story that lends itself to a visual treatment. When deciding on a story, always ask yourself, "What do I see? What do I see?" "What do I see?" If you can't come up with an exciting answer, chances are it's not a very visual story. Some stories simply do not lend themselves to a visual telling.

Please begin to conduct your own research and to propose your own story. Please see https://videojournalismworkshops.com/student-work, to watch the videos made by your predecessors. All these videos were made by previous participants in this workshop. You can also visit Vimeo, search for the channel, Backpack Journalist, and watch many more videos produced during my workshops. Or go to YouTube and search for my channel, Drastiquin. Then watch some of the videos there.

Does it matter that you select a story idea that already has been done? Not really. You can always do something fresh even though somebody has worked there before you. And you can always find new characters through which you can tell the story.

So please remember that these are "character-driven" documentaries. The best stories are told through the prism of one person's experience. One teacher's experience. One doctor's experience. One team's experience. One platoon's experience. So part of your task will be to tell your story through the prism of a character that you select. A character that embodies the theme that you want to explore.

We will continue to discuss story ideas, characters and assignments at the workshop. But we will hit the ground running, shooting on the first day. So the sooner you nail down your project idea, the more you will get out of the experience.

Please focus on this asap. Dig down into yourself for an issue that is important to you. Go to the Internet and do some research. There are some 7,000 non-governmental organizations (NGOs) and non-profits here in the DC area, all with their own mission and expertise. Most of them are delighted to work with us, as we generate publicity that they rarely can afford to purchase. If you don't already have a story idea, select an NGO or non-profit that has meaning to you. And make the contacts regarding permission to shoot there.

Please get back with me with a story idea that you want to pursue. It is imperative that each of you decides on a story that you want to execute during our four-day encounter. Your success during this endeavor will be a function, in part, of how well prepared you come to the workshop.

Please contact me with questions. I look forward to working with you.

Best regards,

Bill Gentile

See what I mean? So as you go about pursuing this methodology, read and re-read the above message that I send to workshop participants. It applies to you, too.

One last thing before we move on. A series of talking heads is not a compelling visual story. Interviews do not usually make compelling visual stories. So if your story idea relies exclusively on an interview, chances are it won't be very interesting.

Proposal, Controlling Idea, Title

If anybody ever tells you that you don't need writing skills in the business of visual storytelling, don't believe them. You will need writing skills from the very beginning to the very end of the process. Your writing is the most visible evidence of how clearly you think. If you can think clearly, you can write clearly.

There is a **progression of writing** that **begins with the proposal** and **ends with the treatment and script.**

We begin with the **proposal**, which is a brief summation of your video project. It's what you send to a producer to acquire his/her approval of, and support for, a project. Proposals should never be over a page long. Most producers are super busy and they just don't have time to read anything over a paragraph or two. I sent the following proposal to the executive producer at NOW on PBS in November 2002. It's long. Longer than it should be. But I was a colleague with the executive producer to whom I sent it, and I wanted to be sure that he understood the overall project. I knew he would take time to read it.

The proposal is your **statement of intent**. It is based on thorough research. It is written in a very **visual** fashion. It tells the reader what he/she will see and hear.

Keep in mind that proposals are designed almost exclusively to get your foot in the door. You just want to open a discussion with the person in charge of the outlet. So you send him/her only the pertinent facts and hope they spark a broader conversation. Here's my proposal to John Siceloff, at the time executive producer at NOW on PBS:

Images of a Revolution
by
Bill Gentile
November 2002

An infant at her breast and a second child at her side, the young woman stands at the head of an open coffin. In the rough-hewn wooden box lies her husband, cut down by U.S.-backed "contra" fighters. Around the coffin stand Sandinista militiamen – local peasants, really -- with automatic assault rifles. They hold stiff, awkward poses, their calloused hands more accustomed to wielding machetes and hoes than Soviet-made weapons.

I made this image shortly after a colleague and I were ambushed while on patrol with members of the Sandinista People's Army near the town of Mulu-kuku on Nicaragua's Atlantic Coast. When returning from the patrol, local peasants said they wanted to show us something. Something important. They took us to a makeshift hut built of logs and black plastic. One of the peasants pulled open the plastic sheet covering the front of the hut and this is what my colleague and I saw. This image never left my mind. Years later, I built the proposal you are reading around this image. And I went back to Nicaragua to find the wife of the fallen Sandinista militiaman.

The woman stares into my camera. Her eyes say, "Look at what has happened to my family and my community." The ever-disturbing picture appears in my book, Nicaragua, a portrait of this Central American nation mired in a war sponsored by the United States.

Two decades after covering the conflict for Newsweek Magazine, I return to Nicaragua to find this woman, her children and the Sandinista militiamen, to learn of their fate since America stopped paying attention to them. In addition, I search for other Nicaraguans pictured in my book, Sandinistas and contras alike, to explore what has happened to them and to their country. I am not a detached observer. I've worked in Nicaragua since the 1979 Sandinista Revolution. I lived there for seven years during the Contra War.

At the height of the conflict designed to overthrow the leftist Sandinista government, Washington argued that the fate of Nicaragua and her people was a matter of U.S. national security. The Sandinistas lost power in 1990 elections and today the plight of most Nicaraguans is, by almost any measure, vastly more desperate than during Sandinista rule. But Washington has turned a cold shoulder to the Nicaragua it once embraced.

What has happened here since 35,000 Nicaraguans perished in the U.S.-sponsored conflict? What has "democracy" brought the people of this country? What have the successors of the Sandinistas achieved, or failed to achieve, since taking power? How did a country once known for its incorruptible traffic cops deteriorate into today's cesspool of graft and corruption? Why has Nicaragua disappeared from the front pages and the television screens of America?

This is the aftermath of an ambush into which I and a colleague fell into while on patrol with members of the Sandinista People's Army. Shortly after returning to the village where we began the patrol, peasants pulled us aside to visit the wake of a Sandinista militiaman.

These are just a few of the questions I will try to answer on my return to Nicaragua next month. More a videographer today than a still photographer, I use a digital video camera to tape encounters with my subjects. I am accompanied by a documentary film crew making a sequel to the award-winning "The World Is Watching," which explores the news-gathering process in Nicaragua. My expenses are paid.

The war over and her two children nearly grown, the woman in the photograph stares into my camera once again. What do her eyes tell me now?

John Siceloff was a long-time colleague of mine. I knew him when he worked for NBC News in Central America. I later worked with him when he produced content for NOW on PBS, which was one of American television's last and best television news magazine programs. He went on to become CEO of Jumpstart Global Media. When I asked John to tell me what he looks for in a proposal, this is what he said:

> *A good proposal does more than advance a story by a millimeter or two. It does not simply "add on" to what others have already done, and done well. And it does not draw a circle around a topic that is in the news, announcing, "That's my story! I'll start shooting and find something there."*
>
> *The best proposals have a compelling story-line, great characters, and a reason for me (and all the viewers) to care.*
>
> - *The compelling story-line. Give me an angle that has not been done to death. Often, the best story begins with a question. Bill Gentile had a brilliant proposal that he pitched me back in 2008. The US Marines are trying to retake a part of Afghanistan that has been the stronghold of the Taliban. Can they do it? Here is the story that emerged: http://www.pbs.org/now/shows/428/index.html The best storylines are a micro-narrative that capture what's happening with larger issues.*
>
> - *Great characters. I tell producers, 'Find me characters that are in the midst of life-changing experiences.' It's not bad if you have someone tell you about a big change in their lives that happened in the past: 'Last year I lost my home to foreclosure.' But it's transformative to follow a character who is in the midst of it all at the moment you are there: on the phone with the banks, packing up boxes, explaining to the kids what happened. Example: this extraordinary story which follows a young woman as she loses her home and has to move out with her small child because of student loans: http://www.pbs.org/now/shows/525/*
>
> - *A reason to watch. Make me care. Make me angry. Make me connect.*
>
> *John Siceloff*
> *www.jumpstartglobalmedia.org*

Sadly, John died of prostate cancer on March 6, 2015.

The **controlling idea** is the essence, the core, the nucleus, of the proposal and your story idea. It's a one-sentence description of your project. It is the central idea, or central thread, of your video story.

Think of a pearl necklace. If you grab and break the necklace, the pearls cease to be a necklace and instead become a swirl of pearls rolling scattered on the ground. The same idea applies to a video story. The controlling idea is what holds the pearls of visual and aural information together, making them a strong visual story.

Without a strong, unifying controlling idea, your pearls of visual and aural information cease to be a story and instead become a swirl of visual and aural information scattered on your computer screen.

If you cannot describe and define your story idea in a single, declarative sentence, then you don't have a firm grip on your own idea and you need to go back and think it through.

Try defining your story idea in a sentence – one sentence -- that begins: "My video story explains…" or, "My documentary explores…" Again, if you can't finish that sentence with a concise description of your story, then your controlling idea needs work. Go back and figure it out.

This is extremely important because everything you shoot or decide not to shoot, every question you ask or decide not to ask, should support your controlling idea. If you have a clear sense of the controlling idea you won't burn up tons of time and tape (or card space) on material that you will never use.

The title of your piece is further distillation of the story idea. Your title either contains key information about your project or it pricks the interest of the audience. The title, "Chain Gang," is a no-brainer.

The **script** is a list of instructions that you design either for yourself or for an editor who will take your raw video/audio material and organize it using a computerized editing program. The script is a two-column document. In the left column is what the audience sees. In the right column is what the audience hears. We'll discuss scripts in greater detail later in this manual but suffice to say right now that **nothing can take the place of the script** in the post-production process. It is vital to organizing a coherent visual story.

The **treatment** is a document that resembles the proposal in that it is a very visual description of what your finished video story actually shows – as opposed to what your proposal intended to show. The treatment typically goes to the producer, as opposed to the editor.

NOTE: This concludes the Pre-Production phase of video journalism. Now let's get to work.

II.
Production

Production: The acquisition of visual and audio materials for use in a documentary or video story.

Ethics & Best Practices

It was the early 1980s. I had moved to Nicaragua and was a photo stringer for Newsweek Magazine. I was still stringing for UPI and NBC Radio. Patrick Hamilton is a Vietnam War veteran and, at the time, was a photographer for the Associated Press (AP) based in Mexico City.

He and I were riding around in the northern mountains of Nicaragua, covering the Contra War between U.S.-backed, anti-Sandinista rebels and the Sandinista government. I honestly don't remember if we were up there responding to specific reports of fighting or if we were just looking for a story. The long and short of it is we came upon a wounded Sandinista militiaman. The kid just hours prior to our arrival was shot through the chest during a firefight with the Contras. And he was dying. So here's what Patrick and I were faced with: Either make our pictures of this guy and get back on the road. Or put him into my 1969, four-wheel-drive International Scout and haul him back over bumpy dirt roads to a hospital in Ocotal, a couple of hour's drive away. If we took the first option the young militiaman would probably bleed to death. If we took the second option we could be stopped on the road by Contra fighters who would certainly kill the militiaman -- and might kill us as well for trying to save him.

Most of the decisions you make regarding ethics and best practices won't be as dramatic as the one that Hamilton and I made that day. But I think this is a good

time to talk about ethics and best practices because it is here, in the production stage, that you will encounter the greatest challenges and temptations.

I learned a very good lesson very early in my career. When planning to move to Mexico to become a foreign correspondent, I wrote to some of the correspondents in the country for advice. These included the bureau chiefs of the Associated Press (AP), United Press International (UPI) and The New York Times. I popped the letters in the snail mail (no email in 1977) and waited.

Scenes like this one were fairly common for journalists like myself covering the Contra War in Nicaragua during the 1980s. Sandinista militiamen in between combat or field assignments resting in hammocks and cleaning Soviet-made AK-47 assault rifles.

The AP bureau chief did not respond to my message. The UPI bureau chief responded in a very brief, minimal fashion. Alan Riding, The New York Times bureau chief and by far the most accomplished of the lot, responded with a long, comprehensive letter that began something like, "Sorry for not responding sooner, I've been on the road lately and never seem to catch up." Alan was the quintessential foreign correspondent. Intelligent. Super-connected. Great sense of humor. He was head-and-shoulders above any of his competition. He was the model of what a foreign correspondent could be.

The moral of this story is that the best of the craft normally are the most generous and the most willing to help, because they are the most secure. They are not threatened. Partly because of this lesson, I've always tried to be generous with people who approach me for help.

Be generous to your colleagues. From a strictly selfish perspective, you should be generous because you generally reap what you sow.

In one of my Foreign Correspondence classes at American University I had a long-time colleague come in to speak with my students. And he warned students to act professionally when dealing with their contemporaries because, especially when you enter the upper stratosphere of the craft, the air gets thinner and thinner. In other words, everybody knows each other.

"I can take any of my colleague's names and, after three phone calls, know everything there is to know about that person," the visitor told my class. And this was <u>before</u> the Internet and social media have allowed us to peek into just about every corner of anyone's life.

Think of it this way: You can spend 20 years building up a reputation for yourself and 20 minutes burning the whole thing to the ground.

If you are short tempered and difficult to deal with, you'll find it hard to progress in this field. I have colleagues who are wildly talented but who cannot find work. Why? Because they are a pain in the butt and nobody wants to work with them. And I have colleagues who are marginally talented but who have work all the time. Why? Because they are easy, and even fun, to work with. Word gets around fast. And if word gets around that you are a jerk, then you're going to have a tough time finding work.

At the 2012 commencement ceremony at American University, former Associated Press (AP) President Tom Curley advised graduates to find ways to work with people. It's cool and romantic to see yourself sometimes as a "lone wolf," Curley told the crowd. But you get more accomplished by learning to work with others.

This is pretty good advice. Especially in a profession that can be so incredibly competitive and incestuous, dealing respectfully with others can be a key component of success.

Take good care of the people who work with, and for, you.

Even more important than your own career are the people who are the essence of your craft – even your survival. These are your subjects. The people you cover. Too often you meet these people on some of the worst days of their lives, when their countries have been wracked by war or disease. When their homes have been ravaged by fire or flood. When a loved one has died.

And too often these people are the most defenseless. The poorest. The least educated. The least prepared. As I learned covering wars overseas, when the scene got really ugly or when I just had enough, I always had the luxury of being able to head to the nearest airport, whipping out my U.S. passport and going home. But the people I covered had no such luxury. They <u>already were</u> home.

And then there are our local colleagues.

I can't tell you how many local "stringers" or "freelancers" were left high and dry after the conflicts in Central America had settled down. The wars ended. The foreign journalists packed up their gear and went home. And the locals were left to fend for themselves.

And especially in places of conflict, these local professionals are extremely vulnerable. Not just the sources who generously share the information that is the grist of our craft, but also the journalists upon whom we rely to get our work done and stay alive.

Too often none of them really know where that thin red line is. During the long, dark days of Central American conflict I interviewed a spokesperson for a local human rights organization. We discussed torture and disappearances allegedly committed by local police and army. The spokesperson was harshly critical of the government. I asked this person if I could use his/her name in my dispatch for United Press International (UPI). As a foreign correspondent for UPI, my work was distributed in newspapers and magazines all over the world.

"Yes. You can use my name," came the answer.

But after a lot of thought, I decided not to use this person's name, out of concern that I might put him/her in danger. My story ran in UPI without the name.

A couple of months later I saw this person mentioned in an article published by an important U.S. newspaper – identified by name. Not long after that, armed men "disappeared" this person, whose remains have not been found to the day of this writing.

I cannot say whether the publication of this person's name was the cause of death, or the straw that broke the camel's back. I can say only that I'm glad I did not publish it.

This section of the manual really cuts to the heart of why we do what we do — and why we don't. I've been deeply unsettled by discussions between some of my colleagues regarding the motivations behind our craft. Do we do it for the money? Or to be macho? Or for bragging rights: "I was there"? Certainly there are elements of this, and I certainly have been guilty of this attitude from time to time. But at the core of it all, the real reason I continue this work is because of the connections I've been able to forge with the people who have allowed me to practice the craft. The soldiers and rebels in Central America who allowed me to tell their stories and to spend weeks at a time with them trekking through mountains and treading mean streets of the region. The *campesinos* who volunteered their perhaps unsophisticated but almost always true-to-the-core analyses of their individual and collective predicament. The women in Rwanda who recounted — on camera — the horrors of mass, systematic rape and sexual slavery during the 1994 Genocide. The U.S. Marines in Afghanistan who granted me the privilege of documenting their far-off war. These are just a handful of the "reasons" that have kept me in the craft since I began practicing in 1977. These relationships, friendships really, are the real "payoff" for long, cold separation from family; for exposure to extended bouts of ugly, ferocious violence; for the loss of friends and colleagues killed or wounded while practicing the craft; for personal lives disrupted by forces mostly beyond our control but to which we must submit ourselves to do our job.

"Don't get into this business for fame and fortune," I tell my students at American University. "Because there isn't enough of either to justify the price that you'll have to pay. Do it for the right reasons," I tell them.

I was telling you about Patrick Hamilton, the Sandinista militiaman and I, up in the mountains of Nicaragua.

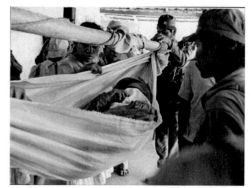

Sandinista militiamen nestled their wounded colleague in his own hammock. Hamilton and I drove him in my International Scout to a hospital in Ocotal.

The rule for intervening or not in a dangerous situation is not to intervene if there are others available to assist. In the event that nobody is available to assist, then it's time to put the camera down and do what you can to help.

On that day in the mountains, Patrick and I slung a hammock inside my International Scout, placed the militiaman in it, and drove him slowly and carefully to the hospital in Ocotal. We left him there, still alive, with doctors and nurses.

By the mid 1980s I was working full-time for Newsweek. No longer did I use black-and-white film. Instead, I used color slides that I shipped to New York.

The Basics

OK, back to Earth.

I'm not going to walk into your professional life and tell you to forget everything you know and to do things my way. That would be crazy. However, I am going to ask you to make a little bit of room in your professional toolbox for the way I do things. I've been doing this stuff for the past 35 years and I've learned from people who have already invented the wheel. So you don't have to re-invent it. If you learn good habits now, at the beginning of this process, you don't have to unlearn those bad habits six months or six years from now and then re-learn the good ones. So learn good habits now and save yourself some time.

Here's something really, really basic, that a lot of practitioners have never learned: How to properly hold a camera. Holding the camera out away from your body is a quick way to wear down your shoulder and arm muscles. It's also a quick way to demonstrate to others that you are a rookie in the craft.

The proper way to hold a camera is to use your left hand as a platform, with your fingers and left thumb free to manipulate camera controls. Keep your left elbow tucked into your left rib, turn your left hip toward your subject. The weight of the camera is supported by your ribs, and your body gives you a lot of support.

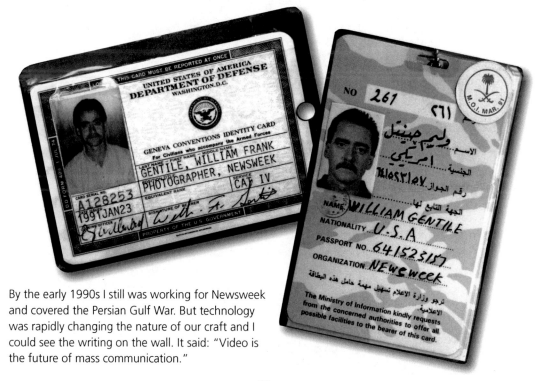

By the early 1990s I still was working for Newsweek and covered the Persian Gulf War. But technology was rapidly changing the nature of our craft and I could see the writing on the wall. It said: "Video is the future of mass communication."

Plant your feet as if you were a boxer in a ring. Point your left toe toward your subject. Point your right toe in front of your body, perpendicular to the left toe. Bend your knees a bit. This stance is much, much more stable than a shoulder-wide stance with the camera propped with two hands. It will not be comfortable at first but you'll get used to it. Holding the camera in this manner helps you to shoot faraway shots and keep the image stable.

I always advise students to use the camera's digital viewfinder only when absolutely necessary, like if you're following someone on a hike or patrol and you want to shoot their feet. Or if you're at a news conference and you have to hold the camera

The left hand should act as a platform supporting the camera. This frees up your thumb and fingers to hit buttons and dials on the body of the camera. Tuck your left elbow into your ribs, so that the weight of the camera is supported by your ribs and hips – as opposed to your arms and shoulders. Stand like a boxer, with left toe pointed toward your subject, and right toe toward the front of your body. Bend the knees a bit. You'll see how steady and stable this position can be.

above your head to shoot over the crowd. I advise them to use the eyepiece instead. You should try to keep both eyes open so that you are aware what's going on around you. You can shift your focus from one eye to the other by squinting. This way you can keep direct eye contact with your subject but you retain peripheral vision and you are aware of what is going on around you. There is no LCD screen forming a barrier between you and your subject.

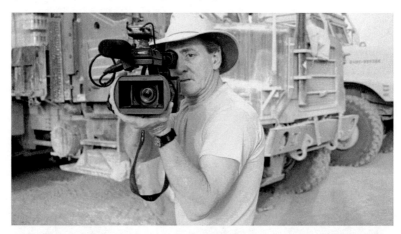

These photos give a sense of what I mean about holding the camera and positioning yourself properly. The two field images were made while I was on assignment with the 24th Marine Expeditionary Unit (24thMEU) in Afghanistan in 2008. Notice that I've got my feet planted in a way that allows balance and mobility. Also notice that I'm using the eyepiece of the camera instead of the LCD screen.

Just as importantly, the LCD screens are not accurate reflections of what the camera is recording. Especially in bright sunlight or with a strong backlight, the LCD screens make it difficult to discern whether or not the camera is exposing for and focusing on your subject or on the area around/behind the subject. The eyepiece gives you a much sharper, much truer, sense of what the camera is recording.

HD Digital Camera

This manual, my Backpack Documentary classes at American University, and my Video Journalism Workshops all are about the visual storytelling language. Not about gear. I've seen people with the latest, greatest and most expensive equipment available come back from the field with material that is absolutely un-watchable. And I've seen others with the clunkiest gear imaginable make films of extraordinary power.

Having said that, it is critical that you familiarize yourself with your equipment. Otherwise, you will never be able to generate on tape or on computer disc what you see in your mind's eye. You will never be able to create the powerful images that drive this methodology.

On the path to mastering the equipment that you work with, nothing can take the place of one-on-one instruction – which is outside the scope of this manual. But every piece of equipment that you buy comes with a User's Manual and I suggest you read it (I know it's a pain) before using that equipment. And take the User's Manual with you every time you walk out your door to work.

What we can do here is introduce you to some of the very basic functions of cameras typically used in our craft. They are listed below.

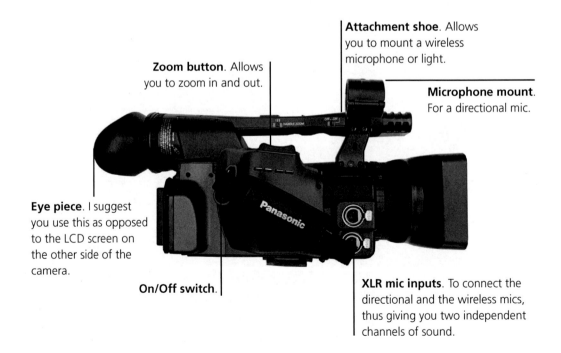

Attachment shoe. Allows you to mount a wireless microphone or light.

Zoom button. Allows you to zoom in and out.

Microphone mount. For a directional mic.

Eye piece. I suggest you use this as opposed to the LCD screen on the other side of the camera.

On/Off switch.

XLR mic inputs. To connect the directional and the wireless mics, thus giving you two independent channels of sound.

Neutral Density or ND filters. These filter allow you to modify the intensity of light and to control depth of field.

Built-in stereo microphone. Avoid using internal mics. The sound you capture with them generally is not good, particularly in situations with lots of ambient sound. Use external directional and wireless mics instead.

Shutter speed controls. Along with iris, or aperture, controls, these allow you to govern the amount of light entering the camera.

Diopter. Every modern camera allows you to adjust the eyepiece to your particular vision.

Battery. Keep them charged and bring an extra.

Focus and zoom rings allow you to focus and to zoom manually.

Automatic focus buttons allow you to focus either manually or automatically.

Microphone controls. These allow you to adjust the volume of sound you are recording.

Gain. Controls the camera's sensitivity to light.

Iris, or aperture, control. Along with shutter speed, this allows you to adjust the amount of light entering the camera to make an exposure.

What Camera Should I Use?

It was a special assignment. Three weeks in the Ecuadoran Amazon. Hiking through the jungle. During rainy season. Reaching villages immersed in a sea of green foliage. Giant, triple-canopy forest above, thick underbrush all around, soggy black mud beneath. I would travel on foot and in dugout canoes, over sometimes raging, violent rivers. To shoot a film about Kichwa Indians and their spiritual relationship with the forest.

I had to make decisions, quickly, on what kind of equipment to take. I had been assigned to similar terrain before. In the early 1990s I stayed for 10 days with Yanomami Indians deep in the Venezuelan Amazon. I had walked the Darien Gap from Panama to Colombia with a colleague on assignment for a German magazine. And during the 1980s I had spent weeks at a time in Nicaragua's tropical highlands, covering the Contra War. But all that was when I worked as contract photographer for Newsweek magazine, and I lugged around professional still cameras so tough that you could almost pound nails with them.

Filmmaking is different. The equipment is more complex. And less sturdy. Video cameras like dust even less than still cameras do. And video cameras hate moisture, heat and hard knocks. As a documentary filmmaker beginning in the mid 1990s, I'd worked in the Sahara Desert, in the Arctic Circle, in Iraq and Afghanistan – some of the most unforgiving terrain on earth. And I always managed to protect my gear even in those difficult conditions.

But working as a filmmaker in the Amazon would present different challenges, and it wasn't until I began packing for that trip in the summer of 2015 that I really appreciated exactly how far the technology revolution had taken us. How much it had empowered us.

No matter what kind of equipment you decide to take on any given assignment, just about every piece of gear has its shortcomings. For the Amazon assignment, I knew that I didn't want to take an expensive, moisture-sensitive camera that weighed a lot and that occupied too much space in my backpack. I needed to be quick and light. But I also needed quality images and sound.

So here's what I ended up taking to the Amazon: an iPhone 6+, loaded with the FiLMiCPro app that I downloaded from the Internet; a "grip" for the iPhone that attaches to a flexible, mini-tripod; a small, directional microphone that plugs directly into the iPhone; a wireless microphone transmitter and receiver, the latter of which attaches with Velcro to the iPhone; ear buds for sound; adaptors that connect all the moving parts; a MacBook Pro laptop computer; an external hard drive to store my media; rubber bands and a roll of gaffer's tape to hold it all together. Oh, and a fistful of big plastic sandwich bags to protect everything from the tropics.

The iPhone 6+ captures high-resolution video and sound. It's got an internal image stabilizer. And with the audio gear mentioned above, I was able to override the internal mic to have more control over the sound.

But like every other piece of gear, there are weaknesses. And these you must understand to either overcome them or simply to cope with them. For example, when outside in bright light, the screen is sometimes hard to read. I wear a hat most of the time when I film, and I can sometimes use the hat to cast a shadow on the screen, enabling me to see the screen a little better. I learned the hard way to use the digital zoom as little as possible – especially in low light – because the image just falls apart when you do. For a better image, you need an <u>optical</u> zoom. Not a digital zoom. And you get the optical zoom with lenses. So it's better to either purchase a set of attachable lenses, or just use the zoom that your parents gave you. That's right, your legs. Stated differently, just get closer.

I made the right decisions on gear that I took to Ecuador. I shot the film, as well as this manual's cover photo and the image with the script in this manual, all with the gear pictured below. My wife, Esther, edited the piece, "When the Forest Weeps." It's gotten thousands of views on the web site of the Spanish-language network, Univision. See it at: <u>https://www.youtube.com/watch?v=Wgqh6PGw1lg</u>, or Google, "When the Forest Weeps."

An iPhone 6+ with a wireless setup for in the field recording.

Character

Let's go back to "Chain Gang" for a bit. As I said earlier in this manual, the methodology that we call backpack journalism, or video journalism, uses character to make the emotional and intellectual connection with an audience. Remember, the best stories are told through the prism of one person's experience. It can be one person, one football team, one high school class, one professor, one platoon. Again, think of Oliver Stone's movie, "Platoon," in which he used a single unit to tell the story of the entire Vietnam experience.

So how do you find character? How did I sort through 400 prisoners in the "Chain Gang" to find my two main characters? How will you find your characters when you head out there to shoot a film?

In the case of "Chain Gang" the first thing I did was stand around. That's right. I just stood around for a while because I knew that some of the guys would not want a camera stuck in their face. Some of them even told me, straight up, that, "If you point that camera at me I'll break it over your f...... head." Hey, I get it. No problem.

Any time we walk into any situation, any space, any room, with a camera, the simple fact that we are there changes the dynamic. Our job is to try to alter that dynamic as little as possible, even though people are going to react to our presence in one form or another.

My challenge during the four days I had to shoot "Chain Gang" was to pick out and to work with prisoners who might be effective characters to tell the story. Some of the prisoners, like the one above covering his face, wanted nothing to do with the film.

So the first thing I did with "Chain Gang" was just to be there for a bit, with the camera hanging off my shoulder, without even touching it, much less shooting video with it. I just let people get accustomed to the idea that there's a camera around and eventually prisoners would come up and ask, "So, who do you work for?" or, "What kind of a story are you doing?" At least I know that these guys are not opposed to the idea of me being around with a camera and perhaps even making images of them. So that's Step 1 in my three-step guide to character selection. **Do they want to be a character?**

So you talk to these guys, figuring out if they pass the second step in the process: **Do they have an interesting story to tell?** You can find people who are dying to be a character in just about any film you want to make but the question is, do they have something to say?

Which brings us to the third step in this three-step guide, or system: **Are they articulate?** While in the prison I talked to a guy who reminded me of that magic prisoner in the film, "The Green Mile," a role that was played by Michael Clarke Duncan. I spoke with the guy for about 45 minutes. We just sat in the prison yard and he told me about life in the south, his grandmother, what he ate to make him so big and strong. He passed the first and second tests. He wanted to be a character. He had a pretty compelling story to tell about how he ended up on the chain gang. But he wasn't articulate. He couldn't put three sentences together. He couldn't tell his own story in a compelling way.

I had to move on and eventually found two terrific characters. One was an African-American from a well-to-do Connecticut family. He started getting into trouble with the law at an early age and landed in the chain gang for fraud and embezzlement. Then there was a white guy who told me that everyone he had come into contact with as a youth were "drunks, drug addicts and thieves. That's why I'm in here," he said in a deep southern accent. He went on to tell me that his father beat his mother "as a regular routine," and that his father was shot to death in a bar where "a man shot him in the back with a pump shotgun for beating my mother."

These two characters passed the three-step guide to character selection:

1. They wanted to be characters.
2. They had great stories to tell.
3. They were extremely articulate.

In 2008 I was contracted by NOW on PBS to do a story on the nursing shortage across the United States. I started with a pile of documents, newspaper and magazine articles, government reports on the issue, studies done by private organizations and public institutions. My job was to produce and help shoot a 23-minute piece in New York City hospitals to explore and explain the problem.

So after digesting all the information handed to me at the beginning of the assignment, myself and two colleagues set out to illustrate all the key editorial points that I knew we had to make. So we cast a very wide net over the hospitals where we had gained access and found the characters we needed to illustrate those points. The resulting piece, "Nurses Needed," was voted the most popular story broadcast by NOW on PBS during 2008. Rather than me talking you through the piece, Google "Nurses Needed PBS" to watch the piece. See for yourself how we use characters to illustrate the points we wanted to make.

There is a fundamental, structural difference between "Chain Gang" and "Nurses Needed." With "Chain Gang" I went to Alabama looking for a way to tell a story that I knew already existed. I just needed characters as vehicles who would tell the story for me. And I found them.

With "Nurses Needed," however, I started out with a concept, with a theme, with editorial points that I knew I had to make. So I had to find compelling characters who matched that concept, that theme, those editorial points.

As soon as I saw Nicole lying in the trauma unit and heard her story about falling five stories from the roof of a building, I knew I had found a powerful character for the video about the nursing shortage in the United States.

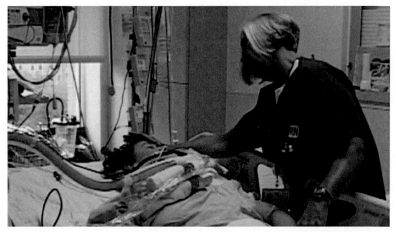

Veteran nurse Mary Grace Savage was Nicole's nurse. This turned out to be an extraordinary bonus. Both Nicole and Mary Grace wanted to be characters in the film; had compelling stories to tell; and were extremely articulate.

We needed a character to embody the high-stress, high-pressure job that nursing can be. When I saw Megan Stack at work, I knew I had our character.

As you move into this craft, part of your storytelling challenge is to find compelling characters that embody the story you want to tell. Any story.

Clips to Story

We already are familiar with the ABCs of the visual language. OK, how do we use them? How do we combine them to make stories? How do you get from Clips to Story?

The basic building blocks of a story are the clips that we shoot out in the field. They are the basic units of visual and audio information that you acquire, or collect, or generate, in the field. You shoot a series of clips to build a sequence. You shoot sequences to build a scene. You shoot scenes to build a story. So the progression is clip, sequence, scene, story.

Another way to think of this is using words on the path to build story. You use words to build sentences. You use sentences to build paragraphs. You use paragraphs to build story. So the progression is word (clip), sentence (sequence), paragraph (scene), story (story).

From bottom up, the progression: Story.
Scene.
Sequence.
Clips (minimum 20 seconds).

As I walk you through the visual storytelling process that we call video journalism, it's important for you to develop a mental picture of structure. Behind the screen of every video, film or documentary, there is a structure. Think of it as an architect's drawing. Normally we don't see it because we're not trained to see it. Or because we're distracted by the pictures and the sound coming from the front of the screen. But it's there, nonetheless. And the more you understand how these structures are built, the easier it will be for you to build them.

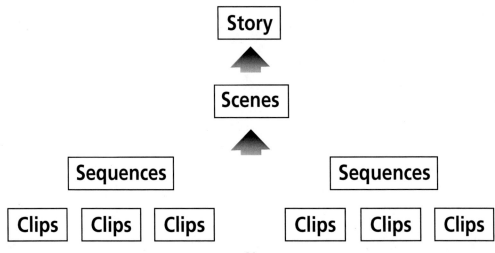

Six-Shot System

One of the most important things you can learn during our time together is how to dissect, or de-construct, a visual story. It's like lifting up the hood of a car and taking the engine apart. Ah! Here's the carburetor. I know what that does. And here's the distributor. I know what that does. And here's the…you get the point.

The Six-Shot System is one component of a broader strategy of de-constructing a visual story. It helps you identify what's important and what is not. What to document and what not to burn up time on. **If you can de-construct a story you can document it (shoot video of it) and then you can re-construct the story in the editing suite.**

The Six-Shot System is a technique. It is an approach. The system is not infallible. It is not written on tablets of stone. It does not always work in every situation. However, when it does work, when you can implement it, the Six-Shot System will help you generate a sufficient number of compelling, coherent images to build a powerful visual story.

And here we begin to use the visual alphabet that we described earlier. The Six-Shot System uses the CU or XCU, MS, the WS, the OTS and the XWS, in this case used as the "master," or "establishing" shot.

Beginners, especially, should never move the camera. Don't zoom. Don't pan. Don't track or tilt. Why? Because unjustified movement of the camera is amateurish. It is gratuitous. And most of the time it results in video that is totally un-useable.

Instead, **make video "snap shots**." Make video snap shots (clips) of at least 20 seconds in length. Yes, 20 seconds for each clip. I want you to make images that move but I don't want you to move the camera. So hold each clip for at least 20 seconds and watch the movement inside the clip. Almost inevitably, somebody at some time will move. Somebody will stop writing. Or stand up. Or walk out of frame. Or scratch her nose. Something will move. And this provides you an edit point, a transition, a place at which you can move from one clip to another.

When you go out to shoot you should come back with a shot ratio of 50 percent XCU or CU; 25 percent MS; and 25 percent WS or XWS. One of the problems I see with inexperienced video journalists is that they wide-angle everything to death. They shoot everything on site but never shoot anything in particular. They come in from the field with WS or XWS but no CU or XCU. They have wide expanses but no details. No intimacy.

So come back with half of your clips either CU or XCU and you'll see the difference this makes in the final product.

There's another reason to shoot CU or XCU. These are the shots you use as "cutaways." You can cut into or out of a scene using these detail shots. You can't do it with WS or XWS.

OK, back to the Six-Shot System.

It's a system that I use and that I try to teach people to use that enables them to get into a scene and allows them to deconstruct the scene, analyze what needs to be shot so they can shoot it and then when they get into post-production stage they can re-construct the scene in appropriate fashion.

I can show you plenty of examples in my own work in which you see evidence of the Six-Shot System but that you don't see every clip that I shot. This is because I've selected only the most powerful images, and I have these images largely because I used the system. If I hadn't used the system, I would not have had the variety of images that you see in the pieces.

Let me explain it this way: Your friend is shooting a documentary about you. He/she is shooting the scene of you reading this book. You are in your office. This scene is an enclosed, contained scene. There are four walls, a ceiling and a floor. You are seated at your desk reading this book. There is a lamp on the desk, pictures on the wall, the usual stuff.

What does your friend shoot? Where does he/she start? What's important here?

Remember this: The best films, the best scripts, the best stories, are not just piles of information that you dump on somebody's head. That's too much information for a person to assimilate, to absorb, at one time. Rather, **the best films, scripts, stories are really "conversations" between the teller and the audience**. You give them some information that poses a question or that somehow pricks audience interest, then you answer that question with some information. Then you ask another question, etc. If you pay attention to the structure of just about every successful television series, you'll see the same basic pattern. It's a formula. They start out by asking, "Who committed the murder?" then give you some information, but then ask another question, perhaps about another character in the show. So you have multiple stories going on at the same time.

If you don't get an audience engaged on an emotional or intellectual level pretty quickly, if you can't keep them engaged, they just move over to one of the more than 500 channels that are available today. Only the most effective stories will engage your audience in a visual conversation. You do that by posing and answering questions.

So what does your video journalist friend shoot when he/she walks into your office? Here's the answer:

1. CU hands.
2. CU face.
3. MS hands & face.
4. WS head to foot.
5. OTS.
6. XWS, "Master" or "Establishing" shot.

Translation:

1. CU of your hands on the book. The questions here is, "Whose hands are these?" or "What's he reading?"
2. CU of your face. Logic tells us that the hands in this clip belong to the face in the previous clip, but just to be sure the next shot is:
3. MS your hands & face. This poses another question: "Where is this person?" So the answer is:
4. WS head to foot of you in your office. We still haven't explained what you're reading so the next shot is:
5. OTS, or over your shoulder down to the book in your hand.
6. XWS, "Master" or "Establishing" shot, which establishes where the previous five shots, as well as others you will shoot, are located.

And that's a sequence.

Wait. We're not done yet. If there are other people in the room, or if you are in a classroom with lots of people, your friend should shoot other sequences of other people in the same room. He/she also should make CUs of any visually defining characteristics in your office. What are they? How about some of the papers and pens on your desk? The pictures on the wall? Maybe your name tag on the desk? Together, these sequences and the individual clips of defining characteristics of the room combine to make a scene.

Remember the progression from "Clip to Story"? Your documentary friend has just gone from clip, to sequence to scene. When he/she follows you around for a few days and builds scenes along the way, we suddenly have story.

This system works best when you are in a place where people are doing a repetitive action. I was in Cuba in fall 2011 doing a story in a cigar factory, and all day long we have a couple hundred people who sit behind desks and roll cigars. It's all day long. It's very, very repetitive. So I walked in and I have 200 people sitting there and I think, "Where am I my going to start?" So I started with creating sequences of some compelling characters. It might be person A or person B, cigar rollers who for some reason stood out.

Take a look at the piece, which Time magazine published on its Web site. You'll see pieces of the Six-Shot System:

Google "Cigar Reader Time magazine" and you'll see what I mean.

The Six-Shot System is a technique, an approach, that allows you to de-construct a scene, shoot it, then go back to your editing studio and re-construct the scene. This system works best if you have the time and you're shooting repetitive action, things happening over and over. You don't have to shoot this in order. You'd be shocked to see how many students come back from their first foray into the field without any close-ups of faces. They all have medium shots and wide shots but no close-ups of faces or hands. This system helps you get the shots you need.

Here's an easy-to-remember list of shots in the Six-Shot System:

The Six-Shot System employs six of the 10 shots that you have in your visual storytelling alphabet. You may not use them all but shooting them guarantees you'll have the necessary raw materials when you edit:

> CU hands.
>
> CU face.
>
> MS hands & face.
>
> WS head to foot.
>
> OTS.
>
> XWS, "Master" or "Establishing" shot.

Bill Gentile's Six-Shot System

Close-Up or Extra Close-Up- CU or XCU of hands on the keys . The questions here are, "Whose hands are these?" or "What's he reading or typing?"

Close-Up or Extra Close-Up of face. Logic tells us that the face in this clip belongs to the hands in the previous clip, but just to be sure the next shot is:

Bill Gentile's Six-Shot System

Medium Shot–MS hands & face. This poses another question: "Where is this person?"

Wide Shot–WS head to foot in office. We still haven't explained what you're reading so the next shot is:

Bill Gentile's Six-Shot System

Over the Shoulder–OTS, or over shoulder down to the computer.

Extra Wide Shot–XWS, "Master" or "Establishing" shot, which establishes where other shots in the scene are located.

Bill Gentile's Six-Shot System

Over Shoulder with Subject. When you generate a number of sequences in one scene, you can make Over The Shoulder shots that connect those characters, as illustrated in the image above.

Composition

I define composition as **the deliberate arrangement of elements in an image**. The key word here is "deliberate." And by deliberate I don't mean that you move things around in the frame as you compose. And I don't mean that you tell people to do one thing or another.

What I mean is that you move yourself, or use a different lens or focal length, or shoot through certain objects, or use people and objects as framing devices, or use depth of field to direct audience attention toward what you are trying to say. Of course, if you don't know what you're trying to say, then you won't know what technique to use in order to say it.

There are a couple of very simple rules that photography instructors use to teach composition. The first, and perhaps the most elementary, is the Rule of Thirds. If you remember a game that we played when we were a lot younger called Tic-Tac-Toe, or X&Os, then you understand the Rule of Thirds. The idea behind this rule is that "placing" key components of an image in the center of the frame is a mistake because it implies no movement, no tension, no interest or energy. In my photojournalism class I define images that place the key components in the center of the frame as "visual death."

In this screen shot that I pulled from a documentary I made in Cuba, the subject is composed in the right one-third of the frame. The Rule of Thirds is visible here, and it is made evident by the red lines we've imposed on the picture.

I pulled this screen shot from a film I made in Burundi, Africa. Once again, the Rule of Thirds is evident.

So whether it's a person or an automobile or a tree, place the key element of your visual message in the one third of the frame, either vertical or horizontal, to give it a sense of motion into the other two thirds of the frame.

The Rule of Multiple Planes is a bit more complex. Think of an image I shot for "Chain Gang," the first major piece I did for VNI when I went to work for that organization in the mid-1990s. I spent four days documenting a chain gang in Alabama. In the subsequent story, I made a shot through the chain-link fence that surrounded the penitentiary where about 400 men were locked up in special quarters for chain gang members. I used multiple planes, or levels, of visual information, the closest to me being the chain-link fence. Behind the fence was a line of prisoners walking through frame. Behind the prisoners was a rifle-toting guard. And behind the guard was another chain-link fence. Four planes, or layers, of information.

You can also deliberately "arrange" elements in an image by using people or objects as framing devices. In a documentary I shot in the fall of 2011 in Cuba, I often used students in class to "frame" the instructor holding the class. There is a logical, organic, connection between instructor and student, and the resulting images are much more compelling than images of the instructor without the context of students.

4. Armed guard in background.

2. Second fence in foreground.

1. Fence in foreground.

3. Prisoners behind second fence.

Remember that your job as a journalist is three-fold. We gather information. We process information. We disseminate information in what hopefully is a compelling and accessible fashion.

We now live in the world of HDSLR cameras. These are the cameras that look like the older single-lens-reflex (SLR) cameras but that actually shoot still photographs and video. The attractive feature of these cameras is the fact that they allow us to control depth of field in a way that we cannot do with regular video cameras. Some documentary filmmakers use these cameras to reduce depth of field and steer audience attention away from all other elements in the frame and toward the exact location that the filmmaker chooses: once again, the **"deliberate"** arrangement of elements in an image.

Shooting Style • Paint With Your Camera

In the mid-90s at a meeting of Video News International (VNI) producers and VJs, I commented to the group that the hand-held cameras making their way to the market allowed us a level of freedom and creativity impossible with the monstrous, shoulder-held Betacams common to television production at the time.

"We can paint with these cameras," I said, and everybody except one person in the room looked at me as if I had six heads.

Of the 100 or so VJs that passed through VNI's intensive, three-week training system, only a handful of us went on to successfully practice the craft as intended. I was one of them. So was the only person in the room to understand what I was talking about.

Look at "Nurses Needed" and see how I shot nurse Megan Stack. We needed to show the high tension associated with the profession of nursing. We needed to show why so many nurses drop out of hospital care. Why they simply burn out. I knew within about 15 seconds that Megan was the person who embodied the editorial points we needed to make, and I knew how to shoot her.

Again, you can find the piece if you Google, "Nurses Needed PBS."

As stated above, the Six-Shot System works extremely well in some circumstances, normally when there is repetitive action. But when action is moving like Megan Stack you have to follow the action wherever it, and your eyes, take you.

Bill Gentile's Rules on Shooting Video

- Position for stability. Left hand supports camera. Use your body as a tripod.
- Keep **both** eyes open.
- Compose as if making still photos.
- Use the Six-Shoot System.
- Shooting ratio: CU or XCU (50 percent) (detail, cutaway.)

    MS (25 percent).

    WS or XWS (25 percent) Establishing or Master.
- Make each clip **at least 20 seconds long**. Count them.
- COMPOSE FIRST. SHOOT LATER. DON'T FRAME SHOTS WHILE ROLLING.
- Compose: The Rule of Thirds.

    Multiple planes.
- Don't wide angle your subject matter to death. Get close-ups.
- Let people walk into and out of frame.
- Shoot what you hear: Radio, music, engines. SHOOT THE SOURCE of ambient sound.

- Shoot what the story is about. Ask yourself: "What's the story now? What's the story now? What's the story now?"
- Shoot the journey.
- Shoot interesting angles. Reflections in mirrors, windows, puddles. Shadows. Silhouettes.
- SHOOT WHAT INTERESTS YOUR EYES. Shoot THROUGH things. Spokes of a wheel, bars of a cell, wires of a fence. Multiple planes of information.
- Be careful with zooms and pans.
- At first, shoot video stills. Later on, move, zoom or pan from still to still.
- Make subjects identify themselves: "My name is John Doe and I'm an electrical engineer."
- Engage your subjects. Elicit comments from them. Remember the Three Magic Questions: "What are you doing now?" "What did you just do?" "What are you going to do?"
- Make subjects speak in **whole sentence**s. "Right now I'm working on …"
- Get your subjects to talk about each other. This develops and enhances characters.

- ANTICIPATE your subject's movements and actions.
- ANTICIPATE changes in story.
- ANTICIPATE Dramatic Arc.
- Be careful when you approach subjects. Your body language sends a message.
- IF YOU DIDN'T GET IT ON VIDEO, IT DIDN'T HAPPEN.
- <u>**NEVER**</u> **SHOW YOUR SUBJECT THE UNFINISHED WORK.**

How to Use a Tripod

I know what you're saying: Shouldn't this section be up in "The Basics"? Perhaps. But I put the tripod section here because I rarely use one and when I do, it's almost exclusively for interviews. Whenever you use one, save time by letting gravity help you. To extend it, hold upright as you loosen the leg fasteners. When you contract it, turn it upside down so gravity contracts it for you.

When you set up, point one leg of the tripod toward your subject. This allows you to move inside the two other legs to reach the camera controls without banging against one leg or another and knocking the whole thing off level.

Also, it allows you to pull any of the three legs (providing they are not connected) to quickly and easily adjust the level of the camera.

Never, never move a tripod-mounted camera by moving the legs of the tripod. Always place one hand on the camera and move the tripod with the other hand. Or simply take the camera off the tripod. I watched, in horror, a person pull a tripod toward himself and the camera, which was not mounted properly, fall to the floor in what seemed like slow motion where it kind of exploded, with wireless mic, cables and pieces of plastic flying everywhere.

Participatory Observation
(or)
Bill Gentile's Rules on the Interview

I refer to my presence as I practice the craft as, "**participatory observation.**" My job is to observe and to document. But I have to participate to a certain degree because if I do not, then the characters I select will not tell their stories. I prefer, and I think the audience prefers, that my characters tell their own stories, as opposed to me telling their stories for them. So how do I selectively and strategically participate in the production? How do I get my characters to tell their stories? Here's the answer: With interviews, both formal and informal. Here's how I define them:

- **INFORMAL**, or on-the-run, interview. Take another look at my, "Afghanistan: The Forgotten War" piece on NOW on PBS to see good examples of the informal interview. These are questions that I ask (at strategic moments so as not to interfere with the military operation) to get the Marines to tell their stories.

And I do this by asking three magic questions:

- What are you doing?
- What are you going to do?
- What did you just do?

If you ask, and get answers, to these questions, your subjects will tell their own stories, and this is always more compelling than you telling their stories. Audiences prefer to hear the characters tell their stories as opposed to hearing you narrate the stories for them.

I chose a strategic moment for an informal interview with this Marine lieutenant about the military sweep he conducted through an Afghan market.

Here are some rules for the INFORMAL interview:

- Get subject to introduce him/herself as soon as possible.
- Engage your subjects. Elicit comments from them. Ask them the three magic questions:
- "What did you just do?" "What are you doing now?" "What are you going to do?"
- Make subjects speak in whole sentences. "Right now I'm working on …"
- Get your subjects to talk about each other. This develops and enhances character.

I define the FORMAL interview as:

- Sit-down. This is the classic situation in which you set the camera on a tripod and ask a series of (mostly) prepared questions.
- Where's the light? This is the first thing you establish upon beginning a formal, sit-down interview. How you shoot the interview is almost totally contingent on the source of light.
- Make your subject look into the light, and into compositional space.
- Make eye contact.
- Get subject to introduce him/herself.
- One-on-One interviews.
- Two-on-One interviews. (you and a correspondent or producer).

- Get subject to speak in whole sentences. The audience (normally) will hear only the answers, not the questions.
- Composition and focus.
- Careful with background. (depth of field).
- Get clean sound.
- Save the hard questions for **LAST**.
- Get written releases **FIRST**.
- Get on-camera releases if you can't get written releases.
- Your last questions:
- "Is there anything I missed that I should be asking you?"
- "What are your greatest hopes and concerns in relation to the subject matter?"
- Do the 60-second video portrait. This is a MS of the subject who merely sits in silence while the camera rolls. This material makes for excellent transitions between interview responses.
- In either informal or formal interviews, know what you want from the subject BEFORE you engage.
- **<u>NEVER</u>, NEVER SHOW YOUR SUBJECT THE UNFINISHED WORK**.

Pre-Visualize, like Ansel Adams

Just about everyone has seen Ansel Adams' images of mountains, lakes and valleys that have become icons of American photography. But few understand how Adams went about his work. And it is from his work that I have learned, and you can learn, how to work more effectively.

Adams used a technique referred to as "**pre-visualization.**" Stated differently, he did not simply roam around the West hunting for compelling images. Rather, Adams had a sense of the images he was looking for even before he set out to find them. He knew to expect a full moon or a half moon. He knew if the rivers were high because of rain or low because of drought. He knew the plants in the valley would be dormant or in full bloom. In other words, he knew what to expect. Visually. He had a sense of the visual possibilities before leaving his house with cameras in tow.

He "pre-visualized." It's something you should do every time you head out to the field. Have a sense of what to expect, so that everything that happens in the field isn't a complete surprise that you have to react to, or adjust to, or catch up to. Go to the field with a visual roadmap in your mind. You'll get to your destination a lot quicker and a lot easier.

The clearer your objective through this process of pre-visualization, the more effectively you will work in the field. So on your way there, clear your mind of clutter. Turn off the radio. If you're traveling with someone, steer the conversation toward the project.

Pre-visualize. Pre-visualize. Pre-visualize.

Sound: The Heartbeat of Our Craft

I sometimes refer to the methodology of backpack video journalism as "three-dimensional chess." Remember the scenes in "Star Trek," of the space travellers playing that game? The table was not only measured by width and height. There were vertical layers of the table, as well.

In our craft, **the first, or primary, dimension is imagery**. The visuals are the essence of our craft. Visuals constitute the first dimension. They are the driving force of our craft. They are the engine inside this methodology. Nothing, at least no story, moves without strong images.

The second dimension is sound. This can be ambient sound or the sound of our characters' voices. Think of the famous scene in the movie, "Godfather." Remember when Michael Corleone goes into the bathroom of an Italian restaurant where he comes out and kills a mobster and a crooked policeman? Go watch that scene today and listen. Listen to the subway train as it rumbles underneath. Listen to the screeching sound of its brakes. Listen to how director Francis Ford Coppola uses sound in this scene to tremendous effect. It heightens tension. By the time Michael leaves the bathroom and approaches the table for his kill, the sound has pushed the audience to the edge of their seats.

In our craft we don't, of course, inject sound that is not indigenous to the scene. We do, however, capture as much of that natural sound as possible so that we can use it to draw the audience into the scene. To make the audience feel as if we are there.

Natural sound has been called the heartbeat of our craft. It is critical that you gather as much clean, useable sound as possible. To do this, I routinely use a camera that has two inputs for sound, one a directional microphone and the other a wireless microphone. I **always, always, always use a wireless microphone** -- even if I have to put the transmitter in my own pocket and wire myself. In the event that the directional mic fails, I have an alternative channel of sound.

Go to my piece, "Afghanistan: The Forgotten War," and look for the wireless microphones that the Marines are wearing. You can see the wire on Captain Dynan as he gives a night-time talk to his Marines. You can see it as he addresses Afghan villagers during a "shurra," or meeting of the local elders. You can hear how Lt. Miller's radio conversations with Dynan and with his Marines make the piece come alive. The sound is building and sustaining the tension.

Captain Dynan's wire

Google, "NOW on PBS Afghanistan: The Forgotten War," to watch the whole piece. It was originally broadcast by NOW on PBS and was nominated for a national Emmy Award.

If I had enough space here I would write the following advice a thousand times. But I don't so I'll write it just once:

When shooting, **ALWAYS wear headphones** so that you can actually **HEAR** what you are recording. Not only can you hear what you are recording, but you also can hear what you cannot see, as sometimes your character is in another room, or around the corner, or mixed in with a crowd. If you hear him/her, you can record important conversations. In addition, you can **anticipate** important conversations or actions.

Here's another piece of advice: When working in the field, never wear those big headphones that cover your ears. They cut off peripheral hearing. You can't tell what's going on around you because you're too focused on (or cut off from) the sound around you.

There are other reasons for not using the big headphones in the field. For example, when I'm covering soldiers or Marines I have to wear the same protective gear they wear. This includes flak jacket, goggles and helmet. And I can't fit those large earphones under a helmet.

So I use the small earphones that kind of just hang in my ears, as opposed to the plugs that you actually stick in your ears. With the little earphones I can hear the sound coming in from the directional (shotgun) microphone and the wireless microphone. And I can still hear what's going on around me. I'm not cut off from my immediate surroundings.

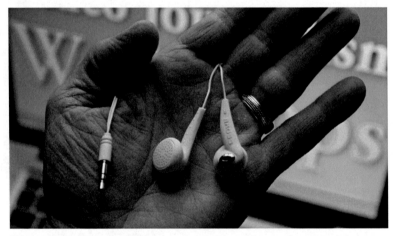

This is what I use in the field every time I shoot. Get a pair at your local electronics store and use them.

So go to Radio Shack and pick up a set of earphones for about $12 and stay connected to the sound that is so critical to your production.

The **third dimension** is narration, which we discuss in detail further down in this manual. For now, let me point out that **narration connects all the dots** of the visual and aural information that you've collected in the field. You use narration not just to explain, but also to ask questions in the "conversation" with your audience. You use narration to set up scenes, to build tension, to summarize and to review. And you use it to mark your work as your own.

What's Behind the Screen?

Behind the screen, or behind any viewing surface be it television screen, computer screen or a cell phone LCD, is a structure. What I want you to do now is to be aware of that structure, to look for that structure **behind the screen** and to not allow your attention to be deflected by the images on the screen.

Whether it's intentional or not, whether well-thought-out or mostly serendipity, every visual piece has a structure, just as every building has a structure. In our business, think of structure as you would an architect's drawing.

Just as we discussed with the progression from Clip to Story, your challenge here is to see structure, to envision your own story's structure, to **DE-construct** a story so that you can shoot that story and then **RE-construct** the story.

As one of my mentors told me: **"The best stories are conversations with the audience."** Not the downloading of information. Conversations. They are give-and-take with the audience – in both the visual and the audio dimensions.

You deliver a bit of information that also asks a question. Then you answer it. Go back to The Six-Shot System to witness the give-and-take conversation. The same holds true with the audio dimension of your story. We'll get into this at a deeper level when we discuss narration.

Dramatic Arc

Dramatic Arcs are just one tool we use to build this "conversation" with the audience.

Watch just about any successful television series and you will see deliberate structure. It may not be immediately evident but it's there – behind the screen. Watch how the makers of the series use dramatic arc as a key component of structure that pulls viewers through each episode, and from episode to episode.

Dramatic arcs are complete stories. Very often they are stories within stories. And don't forget that every story has three components: A beginning, a middle and an end.

Think of "The Sopranos." One episode starts out with the story of Character "A" facing a dilemma. The episode continues with a Character "B" facing another dilemma, which may be quickly resolved. Toward the end of the same episode Character "A" resolves his/her dilemma but Character "C" shows up with a different dilemma that bleeds over into next week's episode.

It's a formula. Again, one of the things I want you to understand about this craft is the structure that exists behind every television screen, or movie screen, or computer screen. Behind every episode of "The Sopranos," for example, is a structure that its creators built and subscribe to. It's a pattern. And once you learn to recognize that pattern, once you learn to deconstruct what you are seeing, you will be able to construct your own.

In "The Voice of Hope" on ABC's Nightline With Ted Koppel, myself and a colleague constructed a number of dramatic arcs with the characters we met at a radio station in Burundi, Africa. This piece is a perfect example of the use of dramatic arcs to keep a video story moving from beginning to end.

It's critical that you understand dramatic arc now, as opposed to post-production, because you must first **recognize a dramatic arc** to shoot it and **then re-construct** it in post-production. If you get to post-production without understanding how to recognize and to cultivate dramatic arcs, it's too late.

Below is a series of screen shots that I pulled from my story, "Afghanistan: The Forgotten War." When the Marines prepared to sweep the Afghan market for Taliban and weapons, I knew I could construct a dramatic arc of the sweep that would help move the broader story from beginning to end. I knew there would be a very definitive beginning, middle and end to the sweep. In other words, a complete story. It is a brief but exciting dramatic arc within the larger drama about the Marine operation in this part of Afghanistan.

So, once having recognized the potential of this sweep to construct a dramatic arc, I went about shooting every component of it. The Marines moved out of their field base and headed to the market. A Marine helicopter flew overhead, providing cover for the Marines on the ground. The Marines blew locks off stall doors to check inside for rebels and weapons. The lieutenant commanding the platoon communicated with his superior about a possible Improvised Explosive Device, or IED. One Marine covered other Marines who sent a mechanical robot to check out a freezer that may have been wired to explode. The Marines blew the lock off the freezer but discovered that the freezer held only soft drinks. The lieutenant addressed his Marines as they took a break after the operation.

By the way, if you haven't noticed, you've just read what essentially is the narration for this part of the video.

NOTE: To see this dramatic arc in the context in which it was broadcast, go to Section III of the script of, "Afghanistan: The Forgotten War," which begins on page 119. This dramatic arc begins on page 131 and ends on page 133.

The Marines move out of their field base . . .

. . . and head to the market.

A Marine helicopter flies overhead, providing cover for the Marines on the ground.

The Marines blow the locks off stall doors so they can check inside for rebels and weapons.

The lieutenant commanding the platoon communicates with his superior about a possible Improvised Explosive Device (IED.)

A Marine covers other Marines who send a mechanical robot . . .

. . . to check out a freezer that may be wired to explode.

The Marines blow the lock off the freezer.

Inside the freezer . . .

. . . the Marines discover only soft drinks.

The lieutenant commanding the unit addresses his Marines . . .

. . . who are taking a break after the operation.

Releases

Below are the release forms I use when making a documentary. These have been vetted by a number of organizations. If you cannot get a signed release from a subject, try to get a verbal, or on-camera, release. You do this by repeating the essence of what the release says – while the camera rolls – and then you ask the subject if he/she agrees to release the material. Make sure the subject responds in a complete sentence, like, "Yes, I agree to allow you to use my image and my voice in your work."

If you're doing news you don't have to worry about releases. But if you're doing documentary you really have to pay attention to this, as a lot of outlets won't air your stuff if you are not covered by releases.

Video Journalism Workshop
Essential Field Manual

Appearance Release Form

Name of "Participant":

Telephone:

Address:

E-mail:

This release is made to allow _____ ("Production Company") to include Participant's appearance in programming produced by Production Company. Participant agrees to appear and participate in the production and taping of the program and to allow the taping and recording of Participant's likeness and voice, conversation and sound, including any performance of any musical composition and biographical information that Participant may provide (the "Appearance").

Production Company is granted all rights and permissions necessary to record, produce and distribute the programming containing the Appearance, and to otherwise license others to use any or all of the Appearance. Participant understands that Production Company, and any person or entity it may license the program to, shall have the right, but not the obligation, to telecast and/or otherwise exhibit the programming, or any advertising, promotion or publicity containing the Appearance in all media, now known or hereafter devised throughout the world in perpetuity. Production Company or its licensee may edit the programming, including Participant's Appearance.

Participant confirms that, to the best of his/her knowledge, any statements made by Participant during the taping and production of the programming will be true and will not violate any third party's rights.

Participant hereby acknowledges that he/she has no right to inspect or approve any or all of the Appearance or other materials produced in connection with this release.

_____
Signature or Participant

_____
Signature of Authorized
Agent of Production Company

_____
Date

_____
Date

Please feel free to photocopy this release for your own video shoot.

VideoJournalismWorkshops.com

Appearance Release Form

Name of "Participant":   Telephone:

_____   _____

Address: E-mail:

_____   _____

_____

This release is made to allow _____ ("Production Company") to include Participant's appearance in programming produced by Production Company. Participant agrees to appear and participate in the production and taping of the program and to allow the taping and recording of Participant's likeness and voice, conversation and sound, including any performance of any musical composition and biographical information that Participant may provide (the "Appearance").

Production Company is granted all rights and permissions necessary to record, produce and distribute the programming containing the Appearance, and to otherwise license others to use any or all of the Appearance. Participant understands that Production Company, and any person or entity it may license the program to, shall have the right, but not the obligation, to telecast and/or otherwise exhibit the programming, or any advertising, promotion or publicity containing the Appearance in all media, now known or hereafter devised throughout the world in perpetuity. Production Company or its licensee may edit the programming, including Participant's Appearance.

Participant confirms that, to the best of his/her knowledge, any statements made by Participant during the taping and production of the programming will be true and will not violate any third party's rights.

Participant hereby acknowledges that he/she has no right to inspect or approve any or all of the Appearance or other materials produced in connection with this release.

_____   _____
Signature of Participant   Signature of Authorized
                                                                  Agent of Production Company

_____   _____
Date   Date

Please feel free to photocopy this release for your own video shoot.

Location Release Form

(Production Company) _____

Production Location: _____

_____

Location Owner: _____

_____

Date of Recording:_____

I agree that _____ ("Production Company") may use the above location for taping the program.

_____ ("Production Company") shall indemnify the undersigned against any property damage to the above location and against any personal injuries caused by Production Company.

I agree that the location may appear in the program and in other programs produced by the Production Company and in publicity about the program and such other programs and that the program and such other programs may be distributed in whole or in part in all electronic and print media now known or hereafter devised throughout the world in perpetuity.

Signature _____

Name (print)_____

Title _____

Address_____

Phone _____

E-mail _____

Date_____

Please feel free to photocopy this release for your own video shoot.

Parent or Guardian Release Form

Name of "Participant":   Telephone:

_____   _____

Address: E-mail:

_____   _____

_____

This release is made to allow _____ ("Production Company") to include Participant's appearance in programming produced by Production Company. Participant agrees to appear and participate in the production and taping of the program and to allow the taping and recording of Participant's likeness and voice, conversation and sound, including any performance of any musical composition and biographical information that Participant may provide (the "Appearance").

Production Company is granted all rights and permissions necessary to record, produce and distribute the programming containing the Appearance, and to otherwise license others to use any or all of the Appearance. Participant understands that Production Company, and any person or entity it may license the program to, shall have the right, but not the obligation, to telecast and/or otherwise exhibit the programming, or any advertising, promotion or publicity containing the Appearance in all media, now known or hereafter devised throughout the world in perpetuity. Production Company or its licensee may edit the programming, including Participant's Appearance.

Participant confirms that, to the best of his/her knowledge, any statements made by Participant during the taping and production of the programming will be true and will not violate any third party's rights.

Participant hereby acknowledges that he/she has no right to inspect or approve any or all of the Appearance or other materials produced in connection with this release.

I hereby warrant that I am the parent or guardian of _____ and I have full authority to authorize the above Release which I have read and approved. I hereby release and indemnify _____ ("Production Company"), its underwriters and licensees from and against any and all liability arising out of the exercise of the rights granted by the above.

_____   _____

Signature of Participant   Signature of Authorized
                                                Agent of Production Company

_____   _____

Date   Date

Please feel free to photocopy this release for your own video shoot.

Materials Release Form

(Production Company) _____

Description of Materials: _____

Owner of Materials: _____

I agree to release the above described materials to _____ ("Production Company") and I hereby irrevocably grant to _____ (Production Company) and its licensees, permission to use such materials, in whole or in part, in any production and that the production, the footage containing the above described materials and any portions of the production or such footage may be distributed in all broadcast and non-broadcast media including, but not limited to television, radio, cable, audio and video, web sites and other interactive media worldwide in perpetuity. I also consent to the use of the above-described materials in publicity and advertising concerning the production and other programs containing the above described materials appearance and in publications related to the production and such other productions.

I expressly release _____ (Production Company), its underwriters and licensees, from any claims I may have arising out of the broadcast, exhibition, publication, promotion, and other uses of this production and the footage containing the above-described materials.

My signature indicates that I have the right to enter into this agreement and to grant the rights as stated above.

Signature _____

Name (print) _____

Title _____

Address _____

Phone _____

E-mail _____

Date _____

Please feel free to photocopy this release for your own video shoot.

Formulario De Autorizacion Del Participante

Nombre "Participante":   Teléfono:

_____   _____

Dirección :   orreo electrónico:

_____   _____

_____

Este documento autoriza a _____ ("La Compañía Productora")
a incluir al participante en la programación realizada por la compañía de producción. El
Participante se compromete a comparecer y participar en la producción y grabación del programa y permitir la grabación de su imagen y su voz, la conversación y el sonido, incluyendo
cualquier actuación, composición musical e información biográfica que el participante quiera
proporcionar (la "apariencia").

"La Compañía Productora" conserva todos los derechos y permisos necesarios para grabar,
producir y distribuir la programación que contiene "la apariencia", y la licencia del uso por
otros de "la apariencia". El Participante entiende que la empresa de producción, y cualquier
persona o entidad a la que esta podrá dar licencia del programa, tendrá el derecho, pero no
la obligación, de transmisión y / o no presentanción de la programación, o cualquier publicidad, promoción que incluya "la apariencia" en todos los medios de comunicación, ahora
conocidos o creados en el futuro en todo el mundo. "La Compañía Productora" o sus licenciatarios podrán modificar la programación, incluyendo la apariencia del Participante.

El Participante confirma que, que es de su conocimiento, que cualquier declaración hecha
por los participantes durante la grabación y la producción de la programación será verdad y
que no se violan los derechos de cualquier tercero.

El Participante acepta y reconoce que él / ella no tiene derecho a inspeccionar o aprobar lo
que sea de la apariencia o de otros materiales producidos en relación con esta autorización.

_____   _____
Firma del participante   Firma del agente autorizado por la
                                             Compañía Productora.

_____   _____
Fecha   Fecha

Please feel free to photocopy this release for your own video shoot.

Forma De Autorizacion De Materiales

_____ (Compañía Productora)

Descripción de Materiales:

Dueño del material:

Estoy de acuerdo en liberar el material arriba descrito a _____
("La Compañía Productora") y por la presente irrevocablemente conceder a
_____(La Compañía Productora) y sus licenciatarios, el permiso
para utilizar dicho material, en todo o en parte, para las producciones y que la producción
y las imágenes que contienen los materiales descritos anteriormente y cualquier parte de la
producción o tomas, puede ser distribuido en todos los medios de difusión y radiodifusión,
incluyendo pero no limitado a televisión, radio, cable, audio y video, sitios web y otros
medios interactivos en todo el mundo a perpetuidad. También doy mi consentimiento para
el uso de los materiales descritos en la publicidad y la publicidad relativa a la producción y
otros programas que contiene el anterior aspecto se describe en materiales y publicaciones
relacionadas con la producción y como otras producciones.

Yo expresamente libero a _____ (La Compañía Productora),
sus suscriptores y licenciatarios, de cualquier reclamo que puedan tener derivados de la
difusión, exhibición, publicación, promoción, y otros usos de esta producción y las imágenes
que contienen los materiales descritos.

Mi firma indica que tengo el derecho a entrar en este acuerdo y para conceder los derechos
como se ha dicho.

Firma: _____

Nombre (letra de imprenta): _____

Dirección: _____

Teléfono:_____

E-mail:_____

Fecha: _____

Please feel free to photocopy this release for your own video shoot.

III.

Post-Production

Post-Production: The stage in which raw materials acquired in the field are edited into a final video project. It is the creative treatment of reality.

Post-Production

Participants and assistants at a Video Journalism Workshop settle down to the post-production stage of the event.

The Post-Production of your video story is perhaps the most tedious but the most gratifying stage of the entire process. As in the other two stages, one of the keys to success is organization. Especially when you return from a long assignment with reams of visual and audio material, organization of your raw materials is critical to a successful outcome.

I return to the **three-dimensional chess** analogy. The first dimension is the imagery you've created in the field. The second is the sound you've captured. And the third is the narration that you write.

The document in which you lay all this out is the script. After the proposal, the script is the second in a progression of documents through which your project unfolds. Your proposal was your intent. The script is what you've actually managed to produce. It is the road map that you or an editor will follow in assembling your vision of the story. In the best of cases, it is as easy to follow as a paint-by-number kit that we used to have when we were kids. The Number 1s are red. The Number 2s are blue. The Number 3s are green, etc. You should be able to hand this road map to a good editor and he/she should be able to follow your visual plan. Of course, good editors will take your visual plan and enhance it. A good editor can take average raw material and make it shine. A poor editor can take brilliant raw material and turn it to mush.

The treatment resembles the proposal in that it is a visual and aural description of what your story will look and sound like. It's written in the same style in which you would write a magazine piece. You hand the script to the editor. You hand the treatment to the producer.

In documentary work, especially, we refer to this stage of the process as the **creative treatment of reality**. This is very much different from the current concept of journalistic "objectivity" or "impartiality" in which journalists adhere to the "he said, she said" back and forth that fails to convey the truth of a story.

Documentary connects the dots. The purpose of documentary is to explain the meaning of raw information. In the best of cases and in the tradition of the early documentary photojournalists like Lewis Hine and Jacob Riis, documentary is designed to raise awareness and to foment action. Hine and Riis devoted their work to shutting down child labor and to bettering the lives of immigrants. In your case it might be to bring awareness to issues of racism, government corruption or corporate malfeasance.

Whether you're doing a documentary or a relatively simple video story, the editing process is utterly fascinating. Multi-faceted. Complex. And challenging. Here's how I do it:

As I review and log the material I've generated in the field, I'm doing a number of other things at the same time. I begin a script, examples of which are included below. I begin writing a treatment, also exemplified below. I have the editing program open and I begin to assemble material on the timeline.

When assembling a story, always begin with the most powerful images that you have. Go to "**Nurses Needed**" (Google, "NOW on PBS Nurses Needed," or go to http://www.pbs.org/now/shows/442/) or "**Cuba's (Rocky) Love Affair with the Harley-Davidson**," (Google the title or go to http://www.pbs.org/now/shows/442) and see that I've begun each piece with what I considered the most powerful images that I managed to generate in the field.

This is worth repeating: **Begin your visual story with the most powerful** images that you have. Especially in today's world of 500 channels and super-short attention spans, you have very limited time to engage an audience on an intellectual or emotional level. If you don't do that in a matter of seconds, your audience is gone.

There are exceptions to this. In my, "**Afghanistan: The Forgotten War**," (Google it.) the story is chronological, because that's the way it made most sense, and the beginning scene, perhaps not the most compelling, was compelling enough to hold an audience.

By the time I sit down at the computer to edit, I've already gone through and reviewed the notes I made while in the field. So I have a sense of what I want to achieve. But video is always full of surprises. Sometime the scenes that you think are brilliant don't really work on the screen. And scenes that you never expected very much from practically jump out from the screen to impact you.

So as I go through my material, organizing and transcribing, I decide which sequences go first on the timeline, which go at the very end and what, more or less, goes in the middle. At the same time I'm writing the script. And I'm writing the treatment.

The Script: Writing to Pictures

I am a visual communicator. I tell visual stories. When I sit down at the computer to build my story, I first lay down images that tell the story. The images are the driving force, the engine, in a visual story. The best visual stories can be told with the sound turned off. Try it. Watch your favorite documentary or video or movie with no sound. If you are able to follow the gist of the story, that means that the storyteller did a good job.

As I lay down the images on the timeline I figure out whether to use actuality from my subjects or clips from informal and formal interviews. If the images, plus the recorded sound fail to tell the story then I have to narrate.

Participants at a Video Journalism Workshop in Washington, DC, deep in the script-writing process.

The scriptwriting process is where the concept of "three-dimensional chess" becomes reality. It is here that you blend visuals, sound and your own words (narration) into a logical, seamless, powerful story.

I cannot overemphasize the importance of the script. In the beginning, you will find it tedious and time-consuming. You will find it hard, and distasteful. You will try to avoid it. Don't! Because nothing can take the place of this document. Only a script will allow you to see words on paper without the distraction of visuals and sound. Only a script will allow you to trim away the excess, redundant and contradictory words of your characters – or of your own writing.

And as you tackle projects of greater and greater length, the script becomes more and more important.

Narration: Your Voice Is a Tool

I hear it all the time, especially from students: "I'm not going to use any narration in my story."

Oh really? Why is this? Why would you decide not to use one of the most powerful tools available to you in the entire visual storytelling process? And why would you refuse to use the component of this methodology that most effectively brands the final product as "yours"?

I'm familiar with the arguments against using narration: "It interrupts the story. It's intrusive. My story should speak for itself."

I disagree. In the give-and-take that this process can be, in the conversation that you conduct with the audience, your narration can be absolutely essential.

In what I refer to as the third dimension of "three-dimensional chess," **narration is the component that connects** all the dots of the visual and aural information that you've collected in the field. You use narration not just to explain, but also to ask questions in the "conversation" with your audience. To set up. To build tension. And to review. To summarize. Take a look at "Afghanistan: The Forgotten War." Go to the part where the Marines are heading into the final combat stage of the operation. It's at Time Code 12:15, and begins, "In early morning light…"

Listen to how I set up this part of the story. Listen to how I inject tension. Apprehension. Listen to the question that I implicitly ask the audience. What is that question? Right. You got it. I cannot do this without narration.

There are other, more mundane, self-serving reasons for using narration. This field can be incredibly competitive and, frankly, somewhat dishonest when it comes to who does what. For example, over the years, I have worked with many producers. Some of them are extremely sharp, talented and hardworking. They can be crucial to the successful outcome of the visual storytelling endeavor.

And others can't produce a decent breakfast. But they hold on to their jobs because they have personal skills unrelated to visual storytelling. This is one of the reasons that I am extremely specific when I list my, or other people's credits. I want to know, and I want others to know, exactly, precisely, what I did regarding any given piece of work. Produce? Shoot? Write? Edit? Narrate? They all are components of the process, and I want you to know which I am responsible for. And narration is perhaps the most apparent, the most tangible, component that identifies the work as "mine" or, in your case, "yours."

Narration can be magic. Read over the following narration from the opening scenes of "**March of the Penguins.**" It doesn't really give the viewer much information. In fact, it really asks more questions than it answers. But it is brilliant. Especially when coupled with the images of the film, which don't give it all away either, this narration is a great example of how effectively your own words can be used.

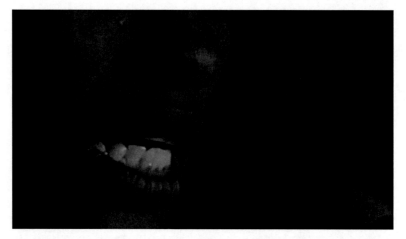

Narration is designed to connect the dots of video and audio information in your story. You use it not just to explain, but also to ask questions in your "conversation" with your audience. You use it to set up scenes. To build tension. To summarize. To connect. To weave in with sound from your characters. To ask and to answer questions. And it's your last opportunity to put your stamp of personal authorship on your work. If it's your voice, it's your story.

TC 02:22

THERE ARE FEW PLACES HARDER TO GET TO IN THIS WORLD BUT THERE AREN'T ANY WHERE IT'S HARDER TO LIVE.

THE AVERAGE TEMPERATURE HERE AT THE BOTTOM OF THE EARTH IS A BALMY 58 DEGREES BELOW. THAT'S WHEN THE SUN IS OUT.

IT WASN'T ALWAYS LIKE THIS. ANTARCTICA USED TO BE A TROPICAL PLACE. DENSELY FORESTED AND TEEMING WITH LIFE.

BUT THEN THE CONTINENT STARTED TO DRIFT SOUTH. AND BY THE TIME IT WAS DONE DRIFTING, THE DENSE FORESTS HAD ALL BEEN REPLACED WITH A NEW GROUND COVER: ICE.

AS FOR THE FORMER INHABITANTS, THEY'D ALL DIED OR MOVED ON, LONG AGO. WELL, ALMOST ALL OF THEM.

LEGEND HAS IT THAT ONE TRIBE STAYED BEHIND. PERHAPS THEY THOUGHT THE CHANGE IN WEATHER WAS ONLY TEMPORARY, OR, MAYBE THEY WERE JUST STUBBORN.

BUT FOR WHATEVER THEIR REASONS, THESE STALWART SOULS REFUSED TO LEAVE. FOR MILLIONS OF YEARS THEY HAVE MADE THEIR HOME ON THE DARKEST, DRIEST, WINDIEST AND COLDEST CONTINENT ON EARTH. AND THEY'VE DONE SO PRETTY MUCH ALONE.

SO IN MANY WAYS THIS IS A STORY OF SURVIVAL. A TALE OF LIFE OVER DEATH. BUT IT'S MORE THAN THAT, REALLY. THIS IS A STORY ABOUT LOVE.

TC 03:59

"But I don't like the sound of my voice." I've heard this one, too. The fact is that very, very few of us like the sound of our own voice. I was a stringer for ABC and then NBC radio correspondent in Mexico and Central America decades ago and it's only until recently that I more or less like the sound of my own voice. Get over it. Your voice is an extremely powerful tool. Learn to use it or take a place in line behind those who have.

Aesthetics vs. Mechanics

As many of you already know, editing is more than just the mechanics of manipulating clips of video and sound through a computer program. The best editors know how to use the visual and aural information you provide them to enhance the message you want to tell. Not to simply deliver information but to deliver emotion. To make the audience feel.

You've already seen "Nurses Needed" as an example of how to use the camera. If not, see, "Shooting Style-Paint With Your Camera." Now take another look to see how the pacing of the edit matches that of the material.

In the same manner in which I shot Megan Stack to underline the high-tension, fast-paced nature of her job, the editor in this case cut the piece to complement the shooting style and the message I wanted to convey. Short, fast clips. Quick cuts. When we move to interview nurse Renee Nicol at TC 06:40, the shooting and edit styles change again – to reflect a different message. Longer clips. Longer cuts.

NOTE: Following is a series of documents that you should find useful. They are part of the paper trail that should be used through the three stages of your video storytelling process. You've already seen the proposal, which is what you propose to do and which you send to a producer or executive producer. It is your statement of intent.

Once you're back from the field, or even while you still are in the field, you put together the logs, the script and the treatment. Below is an example of the way I used to do logs. During and after an assignment, I watch all the material in real time, transcribe every word of actuality on tape or memory card and all the interviews, and make notes alongside Time Codes (TC) about content. On the far right is a rating scale that runs from 1 (not useable) through 10 (very useable) all the way to USE.

Today's video editing programs like Adobe Premier allow you to log right in the computer, eliminating the need for this exercise. But you still need to put together a transcript, which is a chronological document listing shots and interviews, plus a script and a treatment.

Logs

Sample Log

2.0 Tape #1

TC	Shot Description	Usage
00:30	soldiers at Kandajar pile out of choppers	
01:58	nice track of chopper past other choppers, plane	USE
03:20	mixed soldiers/civies move out to Chinook	
04:51	soldiers move toward Chinook	8
09:04	Tomas looking forlorn out window of chopper	
10:00	cu Tomas making pictures out chopper window	USE
11:10	ms Tomas	USE
13;07	cu Tomas and pan to soldiers talking	USE
14:00	soldier hands on weapon and pan to face	use
16:28	nice mountains going by	USE

17:50	Qalat comes into view	
20:00	shot of chopper from our during landing at Lagman, north of Qalat.	
21:35	chopper suspended in air and soldier runs into our chopper	use
22:11	chopper lifts as our own takes off	
23:12	Tomas shoots out window as passenger looks on	use
27:12	soldier silhouetted against passing mountains	use
27:43	machine gun foreground, mountains back. Pan up.	USE
28:52	machine gun and soldier silhouette, mountains back	USE
29:30	same	USE
29:48	best of all	USE
30:30	singing at shurrah. Ws attendees	10
31:26	tribal leader addresses shurrah	
33:15	ws same guy	10
33:26	cu fighter foreground, others back	10
34:40	ws fighters pan up to one fighter	10
35:20	cu fighter zoom out and pan to others sitting	10
36:26	ms fighters zoom to gun	use
36:50	fighters zoom and pan to single guy	use
37:20	ws elder speaking	
37:20	pan along sitting fighters	Use
38:40	cu to zoom faces	Use
39:33	cu fighter face	Use
40:13	outside shot of tent	
40:44	pan of valley	

Scripts • When the Forest Weeps

NOTE: This is the script I wrote during post-production of "When the Forest Weeps." You can see one version of that story here: https://www.youtube.com/watch?v=Wgqh6PGw1lg

"When the Forest Weeps"

Version:	11 September 2015
Date Submitted:	
Correspondent:	Bill Gentile
Videojournalist:	Bill Gentile
Editor:	Esther Gentile
Executive Producers:	Robert Albro, Eric Hershberg

"When the Forest Weeps" examines how Ecuador's Kichwa Indians struggle as their deep spiritual relationship with the Amazonian rain forest diminishes in a clash with the forces of so-called modernity.

Opening shots moving through the forest and begin to hear David singing.	David Nat SOT:

Tod Swanson, David and "witnesses" walking into forest. Pan shots of trees, plants, animals.

Tod Nat SOT: "The forest with all its species is like where the memory is stored…the external hard drive…The memory is not in their head. The history is recorded in the trees, in the land. And so when they go out in the forest, that's when the memory comes alive. The songs that they have are in response to the species. The humor that they have is in response to the species. The stories, the history is in response to what they see out there."

Tod translates David's testimony on how the forest "gets sad" when big trees are cut down.

Tod Nat SOT: David says that these large trees are the owners of the forest. So these large trees are the homes of the forest people. The sacharuna, sachawari. So when you cut down the trees. They get sad because they lose their homes and they go away looking for other places farther away where there are large trees. And they are the ones keeping the forest alive. So you get what we call in English, the 'empty forest syndrome,' where the animals and the plants disappear."

Tod walking along the river path at Iyarina Lodge.

V.O. DR. TOD SWANSON TEACHES AT ARIZONA STATE UNIVERSITY. HE OWNS A RESERVE DEEP IN ECUADOR'S AMAZONIAN RAIN FOREST. IT'S LOCATED AT THE VERY INTERSECTION OF INDIGENOUS RELIGION, OR SPIRITUALITY, AND THE ENVIRONMENT.

Collage of images while Tod explains what he's doing there. Students, instructors, outdoor classes.

Tod Nat SOT: "I wanted to create a place where we could bring together graduate students and like-minded faculty, working on a whole variety of issues, in an interdisciplinary way, around the knowledge that comes from the forest. Biologists, anthropologists, linguists."

Tod at the table with Elodia's ceramics and students standing around.

Tod Nat SOT: "And the focus would be on the indigenous people we would bring to the site, and you have to have forest around it."

Tod points to ceramic bown and camera pans right to Napo River.

Tod Nat SOT: "So what we see here in the middle is the river, this white, this is the yakulindus, which is the bank of the river…"

Elodia paints ceramics and takes them to fire with baby Iyamaji in tow.	V.O. SWANSON CALLS THE KICHWA INDIANS WHO WORK AT HIS RESERVE, "NARRATORS," OR "WITNESSES." THEY EXPLAIN HOW THEIR WORLDVIEW, THEIR IDENTITY, AND THEIR HAPPINESS, ALL ARE TIED TO THEIR RELATIONSHIP WITH THE FOREST.
Women firing ceramics and Tod interview.	Tod Nat SOT: "People who live off the land, who don't have much technology, and who believe that the plants and animals are alive, and not alive in just some sappy way but plants and animals that are dangerous, that can get angry, that can fall in love, all different kinds of things…people who live in relation to the natural world in a way that has been lost to some extent in the … technological world."
Tena tourism signs and outlets: Misahualli Internet café: loggers, "slash and burn" fields.	V.O. BUT THAT RELATIONSHIP IS UNDER SIEGE. NEARBY, TOURISM GROWS. YOUTH FLOCK TO THE INTERNET. THE FOREST IS IRRESISTIBLE, OFFERING INCOME TO THE POOR. LAND TO THE LANDLESS.
Belgica with Tod and graduate students as she types on the computer.	V.O. SWANSON HIMSELF IS AN AGENT OF CHANGE. HE STRUGGLES TO PRESERVE ANCIENT LANGUAGE AND CUSTOM, BUT INTRODUCES MODERN IDEAS AND TECH-NOLOGY. V.O. ALL OF THESE FORCES CONSPIRE TO DIMINISH THE FOREST ITSELF, AND THE INDIANS' DEEP SPIRITUAL RELATIONSHIP WITH IT. ESPECIALLY THE MEN.
Tod interview while Belgica paints David's face.	Tod Nat SOT: "It's been harder for men to hold on to their connection to the land, in some ways, than for women. Traditionally, the family was kind of a complementary exchange between male tasks and female tasks. That was one of the things that impressed me about David. His face was painted beautifully with these patterns that would be the patterns of the hunter and the fisher and a man would use who lived off the forest. And he said, 'It used to be that young women … would be attracted to men whose faces were beautifully paint-

	ed' like his was painted. He said, 'It used to be, that those girls would look for a man who was a good hunter.' And then he said, 'But not now. What young women want now is a man with an education. A man who can get a good job. A man who could have a house. A man who could buy a car.' That's really where the power to provide is. That's the security now. A man with education."
Tod and David gather branches for the sweeping, then performs the ritual. David performs the sweep.	V.O. TOD SWANSON'S 12-YEAR-OLD SON IS SICK AND HE'S ASKED DAVID TO "SWEEP" THE BOY OF ILLNESS. TRADITIONALLY A MALE TASK, EVEN THIS IS CHALLENGED BY MODERNITY.
Tod is hunched over his son.	Tod Nat. SOT: "What kind of pain do you feel right now? Did you take an ibuprofen? V.O. IF DAVID NEGOTIATES HIS RELATIONSHIP WITH THE FOREST, OTHER KICHWA INDIANS BARRICADE THEMSELVES INSIDE IT.
Shot of Bobonaza River.	V.O. JUST A FEW HOURS FROM SWANSON'S RESERVE IS SARAYAKU.
Gerardo pilots boat down river	V.O. I GOT TO KNOW SARAYAKU THROUGH THIS MAN, GERARDO GUALINGA. HE'S THE CHIEF OF SECURITY HERE.
Gerardo explains his community as we see him walk across river foot bridge, young people in school, etc.	Gerardo Nat. SOT: "Sarayaku is a Kichwa community with a territory of 135,000 hectares of virgin forest. We are absolute owners of our territory. We are 1,200 inhabitants. We have seven schools, seven communities, a high school. We call ourselves an autonomous territory. "
Sarayaku village "Centro."	V.O. THE COMMUNITY IS BOUND TOGETHER BY ITS NON-VIOLENT RESISTANCE TO THE ECUADORAN GOVERNMENT AND FOREIGN OIL COMPANIES THAT WANT TO DRILL FOR OIL HERE.
Gerardo's extended family.	V.O. I STAYED WITH GERARDO'S EXTENDED FAMILY. HIS 92-YEAR-OLD FATHER IS A SHAMAN, OR HIGH PRIEST. IT WAS FROM PEOPLE LIKE HIS FATHER THAT GERARDO LEARNED REVERENCE FOR THE FOREST.

Gerardo interview.

Gerardo Nat SOT: "They are the messengers that tell us to protect nature. They know, they see the visions in the mountains, how the mountains are connected spiritually, like a spider web, that protect us. There are people who we can't see with our eyes. There are people who live there, the king of the jungle, or the god of the jungle, as we call him, the 'furi furis' who live in the lagoons. They are people who protect us, live spirits, who protect us. The big trees, there are thousands of living spirits, they are sacred for us. We cannot allow them to be destroyed."

Kids play with a picture book at Gerardo's open-air dining room.

V.O. IT'S AN IMPORTANT DAY IN SARAYAKU.

Gerardo on the radio.

V.O. GERARDO COORDINATES A MEETING BETWEEEN COMMUNITY LEADERS AND THEIR ATTORNEY TO DISCUSS STRATEGY IN THE STRUGGLE TO KEEP THE GOVERN-MENT AND THE OIL CORPORATIONS OUT.

Community president speaks at council meeting.

President Nat SOT: "Sarayaku is living the threat of oil companies. Indigenous peoples must propose achieving an official presence."

Lawyer speaks.

Lawyer Nat SOT: "The other issue is that of the prior consultation. It is something we should insist and put more emphasis on. We have had problems with the entry of these people to make a study of the environmental impact."

Images from Lou DeMatteis book, "Crude Reflections," showing environmental damage, young boy with webbed hand.

V.O. GERARDO AND MOST OF THE KICHWA UNDERSTAND WHAT HAPPENED JUST NORTH OF HERE, WHERE OIL COMPANIES SPOILED 1,500 SQUARE MILES OF VIRGIN RAIN FOREST. OIL PROVIDED JOBS. BUT RUINED LIVES.

Kids play "tug of war" in El Centro.

Children play soccer on foot bridge spanning Bobonaza River.

Gerardo Nat SOT: "They want to destroy this to get fast money from it. (But) even if you have millions, the money will run out. (However) this forest where we are standing and where we will die, will last until the end of time. For us, the good way of living is to maintain the forest intact, animals that we can hunt. The library and the pharmacy that we have here in the forest. That's what's important for us."

Families fishing on the Bobonaza River.

V.O. WHAT GERARDO CALLS, "THE GOOD WAY OF LIVING," IS EMBODIED IN ECUADOR'S RECENTLY REVISED CONSTITUTION. IT CALLS FOR A NEW FORM OF PUBLIC CO-EXISTENCE, IN DIVERSITY AND IN HARMONY WITH NATURE.

V.O. AND UNLIKE DAVID, GERARDO IS MILITANT ABOUT RESISTING THE OIL AND THE TIMBER INDUSTRIES.

Gerardo interview

Gerardo Nat SOT: "They will have to assassinate all of us to enter here. As long as we are alive we will not permit it. Even if they send the best army in the world."

We return to slow, gentle scenes of jungle and to Tod's initial venture to the forest with David.

Swanson Nat SOT: "They say that if you walk in the forest regularly…they say that the forest knows you and not just that you know the forest. In time you take on the odor of the forest. You get the look of the forest, and then the animals and the birds aren't afraid."

V.O. SWANSON CALLS THIS COMMUNION WITH THE FOREST, "THE SHARED SELF." AND IT MEANS, WHEN YOU ARE ONE WITH THE FOREST, THE FOREST REJOICES. BUT WHEN YOU ARE NOT, THE FOREST WEEPS.

David finishes his song.

David Nat SOT.

V.O. THIS IS BILL GENTILE, REPORTING.

ENDIT

Scripts • The Cigar Reader

NOTE: My wife, Esther, and I produced and shot this piece for Time.com while I taught in Cuba during fall semester of 2011. I wrote the transcript and narrated the story. Esther edited the story. Google, "The Cigar Reader Time Magazine" to see it.

The Cigar Reader

Version:	Final Version
Date Submitted:	Tuesday 14 February 2012
Correspondent:	Bill Gentile
Story Producer:	Esther Gentile
Editor:	Esther Gentile
Air Date:	
TRT:	00:04:26

ws rollers at their tables	V.O. THE CORONA CIGAR FACTORY IN HAVANA IS THE LARGEST CIGAR MANU-FACTURER IN CUBA.
Row after row of rollers	
Sequence of girl rolling	V.O. HOUR AFTER HOUR, DAY AFTER DAY, WORKERS HERE TOIL OVER SOME OF THE FINEST CIGARS IN THE WORLD.
Ls zoom out Oladys reading at her desk as the sound of her voice comes up	V.O. ABOVE THE DIN OF THIS MASS PRODUCTION MACHINE RISES A SINGLE VOICE -- THAT OF THE READER.
Odalys to camera	TC 00:00:36 Odalys: "I am the cigar factory reader. In other words, I'm the person who reads to the workers, three times a day for 30 minutes each." 00:00:48

SOUND UP OF HER READING THE NEWS

V.O. EVERY DAY ODALYS DE LA CARIDAD LARA REYES READS NATIONAL AND INTER-NATIONAL NEWS, SPORTS AND CULTURAL EVENTS, AND TELEVISION PROGRAMMING. SHE'S BEEN DOING IT FOR FIFTEEN YEARS.

SOUND UP: Odalys with coworkers

Odalys works and make the rounds

V.O. WHEN SHE'S NOT BELTING OUT THE DAY'S HEADLINES, ODALYS IS LIASON BETWEEN FACTORY MANAGEMENT AND WORKERS, AND, AT TIMES A COUNSELOR TO SOME OF THE 600 CUBANS WHO WORK HERE.

Odalys walks around, counseling co-workers

TC 00:01:41 "Some of them ask for information about housing, for advice about their family problems, problems with their partners or their kids..." 00:01:53

TC 00:02:04 "You have to be able to keep the secrets of people who trust you and come to you for help." 00:02:11

Sound up of her reading

V.O. SHE PROVIDES INFORMATION ABOUT FOOD RECIPES, SEXUALITY AND BIRTH CONTROL, PSYCHOLOGY AND CHILD REARING. SHE READS THE OFFICIAL GOVERNMENT NEWS.

Odalys interacts with the workers, walking and talking.

Checking Romeo y Julieta boxes sequence

V.O. SHE ALSO READS CLASSICS LIKE "ROMEO AND JULIET," WHICH IS WHERE THIS CUBAN CIGAR GETS ITS NAME.

Pictures of Odalys reading

V.O. LIKE CIGAR-MAKING ITSELF, THIS JOB HAS DEEP ROOTS HERE, DATING BACK BEFORE RADIO OR RECORDED SOUND.

Pictures from Library of Congress

V.O. DURING THE WAR OF INDEPEN-DENCE FROM SPAIN, READERS LED THE DRIVE FOR MONEY TO FUND CUBA'S STRUGGLE FOR LIBERATON.

Odalys reading at the podium

Man at press

V.O. PARTLY BECAUSE OF THIS PROUD TRA-DITION, CUBA IS ONE OF THE FEW COUN-TRIES WHERE READERS STILL EXIST.

V.O. TODAY, ODALYS IS ONE OF ABOUT ONE HUNDRED READERS STILL WORKING IN FACTORIES ACROSS THIS CARIBBEAN ISLAND.

Afro-Cuban guy with the cell phone.

Odalys interacts with the workers, walking and talking.

V.O. PORTABLE, ELECTRONIC GADGETS ARE INCREASINGLY AVAILABLE HERE. BUT ODALYS SAYS HER JOB IS AS SECURE AS THE CIGAR MAKERS THEMSELVES.

We see Odalys making the rounds, talking and joking with people.

TC 00:03:48 "Modern appliances cannot replace the readers, because the reader is a living person who walks, who converses, and this can't be replaced by anything or anybody." 00:04:00

The sign on the backof Odalys' chair says, "READER."

Overhead shot of man rolling next to machine, the CU hands rolling.

TC 00:04:03 "Because no machine, for example, can substitute the handiwork of man, understand? 00:04:14

TC 00:04:16 "No machine can make a cigar as perfect as a properly trained human be-ing can make it."

Odalys closes the newspaper she's been reading.   Nat Sound.

END

Scripts • Harley-Davidson

NOTE: I produced and shot this piece for Time.com while I taught in Cuba during fall semester of 2011. I wrote the transcript and narrated the story. My wife, Esther, edited the piece. Google "Harley-Davidson Cuba Time Magazine" to see it.

Harley-Davidson

Version:	#1
Date Submitted:	22 March 2012
Correspondent:	Bill Gentile
Story Producer:	Bill Gentile
Editor:	Esther Gentile
Approval:	
Air Date:	
TRT:	

Bikers arrive at restaurant	V.O. THIS IS NOT JUST ANOTHER MOTOR-CYCLE CLUB.
Adolfo on the highway with flag on bike	V.O. IT'S THE LATIN AMERICAN MOTORCY-CLE ASSOCIATION. AND THIS IS CUBA.
Adolfo pulls up to restaurant	Nat SOT (TC 00:22) "If I have the possibility to choose, I choose a Harley. The Harley, for me, is my passion. It's what I like. For me it's the best motorcycle." (00:34)
	V.O. ASSOCIATION PRESIDENT ADOLFO PRIETO IS REFERING TO HIS 1958 HARLEY-DAVIDSON.
Bikers assemble on street	V.O. ABOUT HALF OF THE GROUP MEMBERS RIDE THE AMERICAN MOTORCYCLE MADE INTERNATIONALY FAMOUS IN MOVIES LIKE "EASY RIDER."
	V.O. IT'S BEEN A ROCKY LOVE AFFAIR. THANKS TO THE US TRADE EMBARGO, PARTS FOR THESE BIKES ARE TOUGH TO COME BY HERE.
Adolfo opens garage	V.O. ASSOCIATION PRESIDENT PRIETO SAYS THIS POSES SPECIAL CHALLENGES TO THE GROUP'S MEMBERS.

Interview and getting out of garage	Adolfo Nat SOT (TC 01:02) "In Cuba, it's not the same as in other countries, where you have an old motorcycle like that because it's a hobby or a collector's item and you only take it out on weekends. Here in Cuba we use them for everything." (01:22)
Adolfo gets off bike and addresses group	V.O. HARLEYS WERE POPULAR HERE BEFORE FIDEL CASTRO CAME TO POWER. CUBAN COPS USED THEM AS THE OFFICIAL POLICE BIKE.
Pan bike "Harley 1954"	V.O. ALL OF THESE HARLEYS DATE BACK PRIOR TO THE REVOLUTION -- SOME OF THEM TO THE 1930S AND 40S.
Old Harleys rolling in	V.O. BUT CASTRO ROLLED INTO HAVANA IN JANUARY 1959 AND THE HARLEYS -- LIKE SO MANY OTHER THINGS AMERICAN -- FELL FROM FAVOR AND GOT SCARCE.
white skull hanging off the old Harley	V.O. RUMOR HAS IT THE REVOLUTIONAR-IES ROUNDED UP MANY OF THE HARLEYS, DUMPED THEM IN A COMMON GRAVE AND COVERED THEM UP.
Screen fades to black	

Old cars in Havana	V.O. LIKE THE ANCIENT AMERICAN AUTOS THAT STILL CRISSCROSS THESE STREETS, KEEPING THESE OLD BIKES RUNNING IS A LABOR OF LOVE.
Adolfo opens garage door	
Sobrino at Adolfo's place	V.O. JOSE SOBRINO FELL IN LOVE WITH HARLEYS WHEN HE WAS A KID, RIDING AROUND CUBA ON THE BACK OF HIS DAD'S BIG TWO-WHEELER.
Sobrino speaking	Nat. SOT (TC 02:21) "When I was three years old he would put me up here and take me around on that Harley. I think it was a Flathead, 1940 or so." (02:30)
	V.O. NOW HE'S GOT HIS OWN BIKE AND HIS OWN REPAIR SHOP, WHERE HE FIXES OTHER PEOPLES' BIKES, TOO.
Sobrino in shop	Nat SOT Sobrino: (02:36) "One of these flanges that was broken, I fixed it with a plate of cardboard. This one is restored. It looks like new." (02:45)
	V.O. HE RESTORES HARD-TO-BUY ENGINE PARTS, SOMETIMES EVEN MANUFACTUR-ING HIS OWN.
Sobrino in shop	Nat SOT Sobrino (TC 02:49) "Sometimes it takes me a whole year to do an engine. I have to assemble them. It's all ready. Here the hardest thing are the tires. These were donated." (02:59)
Max in his shop	V.O. TODAY HE IS FIXING A HARLEY OWNED BY AN ITALIAN WHOS'S LIVED IN HAVANA FOR YEARS.
Max in Adolfo's shop with Harley	Nat SOT Max: (TC 03:07) "When you start it, it sticks." (03:11)
Max driving in Old Havana and Malecon	V.O. THANKS TO DEDICATED MECHAN-ICS LIKE SOBRINO, CUBA'S PASSION FOR HARLEY-DAVIDSON LINGERS ON.

Picture of Che poster at Piragua	V.O. HARLEY FANS EVEN APPROPRIATE REVOLUTIONARY ICON CHE GUEVARA, TO SHOW DEVOTION TO THEIR MOTOR-CYCLES.
Various scenes from Malecon	V.O. ON SATURDAYS THESE HARLEY AFI-CIONADOS SHOW UP AT THIS HAVANA HANGOUT TO SEE AND BE SEEN, AND TO SHARE THEIR PASSION FOR THEIR BIKES.
People gawking at the bikes	V.O. THESE OLD MOTORCYCLES NOW ARE AN ATTRACTION FOR FOREIGN TOURISTS AND LOCAL WANNA-BEES.
Girl and boyfriend at Piragua	V.O. HERE, EVEN IF YOU'VE NEVER OWNED A HARLEY, YOU CAN PRETEND THAT YOU DO.OR AT LEAST, THAT YOUR BOYFRIEND DOES.
	V.O. FOR TIME VIDEO, THIS IS BILL GENTILE, IN HAVANA, CUBA.

ENDIT

Scripts • Afghanistan: The Forgotten War

NOTE: I pitched, shot, produced, wrote and narrated this piece for NOW on PBS during and after a three-week embed with the 24th Marine Expeditionary Unit (24th MEU) in May-June 2008. The story was nominated for a national Emmy Award and competed into the final round of selection. To see it, you can Google, "NOW on PBS Afghanistan: The Forgotten War," or you can watch it here: http://www.pbs.org/now/shows/428

A script is a document that you hand to an editor, along with the raw material, and he/she should be able to put together your video story. The initial stage is rather like a paint-by-numbers landscape. Blue for Number 1. Green for Number 2. Red for Number 3, and so forth. As the piece takes form, a good editor (hopefully working in conjunction with you) should be able to make the piece even better than you had envisioned. A bad editor, on the other hand, is capable of taking brilliant material and making it un-watchable.

As you will see, I identified the material by the numbered "batches" that I down-loaded into an external hard drive from the Sony EX-1 that I used in Afghanistan. To a degree, we all create our own system to organize our material in the field. You can organize your material in numbered, chronological batches, as I do. You can organize your material by subject. Whatever system you develop and use, you <u>must</u> organize – which is one of the keys to the post-production stage. Especially when you come in from the field with dozens and dozens of hours of material, if you fail to properly organize, you will fail to access the material in a timely, effective manner. Stated differently, some of the best of your work could end up on the cutting room floor – permanently – simply because you cannot find, or don't remember it.

So in this script, you will see, for example: "17.Alpha TC 26:00 Marines dig burn pit." This means "media batch number 17 of Alpha Company material at Time Code 26:00 where we see Marines dig burn pit." This was one of the ways in which I've learned to organize material. Now, however, I do most of this work in the video editing software.

Afghanistan: The Forgotten War

Version:	1
Date:	Friday 18 July 2008
Correspondent:	Bill Gentile
Story Producer:	Bill Gentile
Video Journalist:	
Editor:	Larry Goldfine
Sound Tech:	
Approval:	
Air Date:	
TRT:	

01.Alpha TC 16:50 Marines on radio planning	SOT: "You have four and a half minutes… I'm looking for air on Target One…I'm gonna put 500-pound air burst over the truck. I'm gonna put another 500-pound GBU on the compound…copy that, 1, 3, 0, 5, 4…"
01.Alpha various.	V.O. THE 24TH MARINE EXPEDITIONARY UNIT HAS COME TO A TOUGH NEIGHBORHOOD – TERRITORY CONTROLLED BY THE TALIBAN, NEAR THE BORDER WITH PAKISTAN.
01.Alpha TC 17:40, 17:45	"Roger. Did you copy four minutes and three zero seconds?

SOT: "First pass they're hitting the truck and then the compound...sweet. I'll take it."

01.Alpha TC 19:38 Air controller confirms strike sequence.

SOT: "Afirm. First pass will be GPA on first compound..."

01.Alpha TC 19:12 Capt. Sean Dynan

V.O. 31-YEAR-OLD CAPTAIN SEAN DYNAN COMMANDS ALPHA COMPANY. THE MONTHS THAT THE MARINES ARE SPENDING HERE ARE PART OF A BROAD STRATEGY TO RETAKE CONTROL OF THE AREA ALONG THE AFGHAN-PAKISTAN BORDER WHERE TALIBAN AND AL QAEDA INSURGENTS HAVE DUG IN.

V.O. DYNAN AND HIS MEN USE PINPOINT ACCURACY TARGETING THE ENEMY.

01.Alpha TC 20:26 Dynan speaks to camera

SOT: "Right now we've identified the enemy doing their re-supply so we're going to hit the ammo truck and we're going to hit the compound they're moving to right now..."

01.Alpha TC 20:16 Dynan shaking head from side to side.

V.O. THERE IS SOME CONFUSION ABOUT THE EXACT LOCATION OF THE ENEMY. THE MARINES ARE CONCERNED ABOUT KILLING CIVILIANS. AND THE AIR STRIKE IS CANCELLED.

01.Alpha TC 20:19 Dynan looking tense and dejected.

Nat SOT.

01.Alpha TC 16:45 young Marine looks up apprehensive

Nat. SOT.

THE MISSION OF THE MARINES REPRESENTS A NEW STRATEGY AIMED AT WINNING AFGHAN HEARTS AND MINDS.

23 May #1 TC 22:20 chopper flies low over equipment at Forward Operating Base Dwyer.

24 May #1 TC 42:52 track shot around Humvees, Marines at FOB Dwyer.

24 May #1 TC 52:55 convoy pulls out.

V.O. FOR NEARLY THREE WEEKS, I FOLLOWED THE MARINES ON THE FRONT LINES OF WHAT HAS BEEN CALLED "THE REAL WAR ON TERROR."

V.O. THEIR GOAL, TO PUSH THE TALIBAN BACK AND DESTROY ITS FIXED POSITIONS. AND JUST AS IMPORTANT, TO WIN THE SUPPORT OF THE VILLAGERS AND GET THE ECONOMY RE-STARTED.

V.O. THERE'S A QUESTION HERE. CAN THESE SEASONED FIGHTERS ALSO PLAY THE ROLE OF PEACEMAKERS AND WIN THE TRUST OF THE LOCAL POPULATION?

24 May #1 TC 06:27 Marines swallowed by dust storm.

GRAPHIC

V.O. THE MARINES ARE OPERATING IN ONE OF THE RICHEST AGRICULTURAL REGIONS OF AFGHANISTAN. THE HELMAND RIVER VALLEY HAS BECOME A KEY ROUTE FOR TALIBAN FIGHTERS, WEAPONS AND MATERIEL FLOWING FURTHER NORTH INTO AFGHANISTAN, AND FOR OPIUM FLOWING SOUTH FROM THIS REGION INTO PAKISTAN.

01.Alpha TC 18:35 ws Marine compound at dusk and Marines walk through frame, and fade to black.

V.O. THIS IS THE OPIUM CAPITAL OF THE WORLD…

V.O. …AND IT'S OPIUM THAT HELPS FUND THE INSURGENTS' FIGHT.

01.Alpha TC 05:14 cu map held by Miller

Nat. SOT. "What's up Lieutenant?" and Miller responds…

01.Alpha TC 05:17 Miller on radio with Dynan.

V.O. 2nd LIEUTENANT SHEAN MILLER WORKS UNDER CAPTAIN DYNAN. MILLER COMMANDS ALPHA COMPANY'S 2ND PLATOON.

01.Alpha TC 25:25 cu of radio.

Nat. SOT. From radio, "Roger, sir, take a squad out and see what we can see…

01.Alpha TC 25:17 ws Miller and others listening.

V.O. MILLER GETS WORD ON THE INSURGENTS, AND MOVES HIS MEN INTO POSITION TO TAKE THEM ON.

01.Alpha TC 25:50 cu Miller

SOT

01.Alpha TC 26:30 Miller in lookout

SOT Miller: "There's a whole bunch of activity here in the north…"

01.Alpha TC 26:50 ms Miller	SOT: "My western post sighted a pickup truck…moving south to north…"
Hatchet shot?	V.O. TALIBAN INSURGENTS SEIZED THIS AREA FROM THE AFGHAN GOVERNMENT ABOUT TWO YEARS AGO.
Two civilians head over the horizon.	V.O. BACK IN APRIL WHEN THE MARINES ARRIVED, THE CIVILIANS HAD ALREADY FLED TO THE DESERT BECAUSE THEY KNEW A FIGHT WAS COMING.
	V.O. IN MAY, AS THE MARINES ADVANCED, THE TALIBAN PUT UP FEROCIOUS RESISTANCE. BUT A RELENTLESS MARINE OFFENSIVE PUSHED THE AMERICANS DEEP INTO THE VALLEY.
	V.O. THIS AREA NOW IS A FREE-FIRE ZONE. ANYONE STILL HERE IS A SUSPECTED TALIBAN FIGHTER -- AND MAY BECOME A TARGET.
01.Alpha TC 27:27	SOT Miller: "Currently in building 59 is where it was sighted…"
01.Alpha TC 27:36	"We're just getting ready…"
	V.O. MILLER GETS WORD THAT A NEARBY SQUAD OF MARINES IS TAKING FIRE.

01.Alpha TC 28:39	SOT MILLER: "That squad that moved out… They are engaged with small fire and RPGs.
01.Alpha TC 32:06	V.O. I MOVE UP WITH STAFF SERGEANT STEVEN VALLEJO. VALLEJO IS A KICKAPOO INDIAN FROM KANSAS CITY. THIS IS VALLEJO'S SECOND DEPLOYMENT. THE FIRST WAS TO IRAQ.
01.Alpha TC 32:36 Ssgt. Vallejo walking to forward position.	
01.Alpha TC 33:04 Ssgt. Vallejo looking through scope.	Nat SOT: radio, "Roger be advised this may be dangerously close to 155…"
01.Alpha TC 34:15 Ssgt. Vallejo	Nat. SOT: radio, "the enemy is loading a small machine gun…"
01.Alpha TC 34:40 Ssgt. Vallejo talks in mic.	Nat SOT: "Apache Two Apache Two this is Lightening…send it Lightening…Roger be advised…"
01.Alpha TC 35:45 Vallejo	Nat SOT: "We also have a sniper platoon up there, which is where we're going in a minute…"
01.Alpha TC 37:21	VO: WE MEET THE SNIPERS LUGGING A LONG-RANGE .50 CALIBER RIFLE.
01.Alpha TC 37:30	VO: WE MAKE OUR WAY PAST FIELDS OF POPPIES…AND IMMEDIATELY TAKE ENEMY FIRE.
01.Alpha TC 38:27 .50 Cal. Over a wall.	Nat. SOT. V.O.
01.Alpha TC 39:20 Ssgt. Vallejo	Nat. SOT: "Is that incoming, sir? Yes it is. That's incoming." V.O. THE MARINES RESPOND WITH ARTILLERY … AND WITH THE SNIPER RIFLE.
01.Alpha TC 41:00 Sgt. Sheets	Nat SOT: "Hey Staff Sergeant. Hey Staff Sergeant…we got a tractor moving west with what appears to be mortar tubes…950 yards."
01.Alpha TC 42:50 Sgt. Sheets	Nat SOT: "You guys got a 153 down there?"

01.Alpha TC 44:00 ls artillery rounds pound field	Nat SOT: impacts.
01.Alpha TC 45:30 Michael looks through scope.	Nat. SOT: radio traffic, "Apache One…"
01.Alpha TC 46:20 ls spotter pan ws Michael	Nat. SOT
01.Alpha TC 46:27 cu sniper	Nat. SOT: "Hey if you give me your best f….. direction…I'll get air on it right now."
01.Alpha TC 46:58 spotter and Michael the sniper	
01.Alpha TC 48:00 Michael	Nat. SOT: "Left point two…"
01.Alpha TC 48:25 nice ls Michael zoom ws & back.	
01.Alpha TC 48:50 Michael fires a shot	Nat. SOT: "Moped. I disabled a Moped… Hey get that other mag up here…see the guy on the Moped? Stand by…"
01.Alpha TC 51:30 Sheets calls to Marine	Nat. SOT: "Hey pull this mag out of the f….. sack…"
01.Alpha TC 52:12 Sheets on radio	Nat. SOT: "Hey Staff Sergeant. Engaged two males on Mopeds."
01.Alpha TC 52:40	
01.Alpha TC 53:04 Michael to Sheets	SOT: "Hey one male on Moped…KIA… possible other…"
01.Alpha TC 56:50 Sheets on radio	SOT: "One individual definite KIA…another hurt…a third engaged…"
01.Alpha TC 00:10; 00:54	V.O. IT'S A DEADLY GUERRILLA WAR THAT GOES ON DAY AND NIGHT.
01.Alpha TC 01:48	"See the impact?" & machine gun fire..
01.Alpha TC 02:14	"Sir this one's coming in proximity…Hey get back…What the heck you doin' down there?"
	V.O. THE NEXT MORNING THE MARINES SPOT INSURGENTS MOVING IN ON THEIR POSITION FROM THIS COMPOUND.

02.Alpha TC 11:34	Miller SOT: "Right now we just had three enemy low crawl into our position in the south...weapons..."
02.Alpha TC 33:20	V.O. MILLER REQUESTS AIR AND ARTILLERY SUPPORT.
02.Alpha TC 13:30 two choppers fly overhead	Nat. SOT.
We see Miller speaking with his men.	V.O. THIS IS MILLER'S FIRST DEPLOYMENT, WHICH MAKES HIM A ROOKIE. THE 24-YEAR- OLD IS FROM AUSTIN, TEXAS. HE COORDINATES THE 40 –PLUS MARINES IN HIS PLATOON, AS WELL AS THE AIR AND ARTILLERY ASSAULT.
02.Alpha TC 13:30	V.O. HUEY AND COBRA HELICOPTERS INITIATE THE ATTACK. THAT'S THE SOUND OF RAPID-FIRE MACHINE GUNS STRAFING ENEMY POSITIIONS.
	V.O MILLER MUST ENSURE THAT NEITHER THE ARTILLERY NOR HIS MARINES ON THE GROUND ACCIDENTALLY HIT THE HELICOPTERS OVERHEAD. TIMING IS CRITICAL.
02.Alpha TC 15:30 Miller running from and to radio.	Nat SOT: "Roger..."
02.Alpha TC 15:49 two Marines head to firefight	Nat. SOT: pull sound of Cobra firing from 15:54.
02.Alpha TC 16:03 Cobra overhead.	
02.Alpha TC 16:13 ls Marines at wall and field afire	Miller Nat SOT: "Hold up...hold up for a couple minutes...I'll tell you when to shoot, alright..."
02.Alpha TC 16:27-16:34 xls to ls Marines at wall	Nat. SOT.
	V.O. ROCKETS FROM THE HELICOPTERS SET THE FIELDS ABLAZE.
02.Alpha TC 16:44 Cobra fires	Miller Nat. SOT: "Three minutes. Three minutes."

02.Alpha TC 17:06 Huey fires	Miller Nat. SOT. "Two minutes. We got two minutes."
02.Alpha TC 17:37 ms field on fire	Nat. SOT.
02.Alpha TC 17:53 Miller runs up to wall	Miller SOT: "We got a minute and a half." Nat. SOT: 18:05 for chopper firing.
	V.O. THE HELICOPTERS PULL BACK AND MILLER ORDERS GROUND FIRE.
Miller's men firing.	
02.Alpha TC 18:15 various Marines at wall 02.Alpha TC 18:40	Nat. SOT: "We got arty coming in, sir. Miller SOT: "As soon as it hits…15 seconds…get the machine gun up…along the tree line…keep it going…"
02.Alpha TC 20:02 Marine running 02.Alpha TC 20:11 group Marines firing at wall	SOT Nat.
02.Alpha TC 20:24 Marines and Miller firing	Miller Nat. SOT: "…40 seconds…40 seconds till air comes back around…get ready to cease fire."
02.Alpha TC 21:45 Cobra reappears	Miller SOT: "That was one heck of a fire there for a while…alright, second run."
02.Alpha TC 23:14 ms Huey overhead 02.Alpha TC 23:55 Marines at wall	Miller SOT: "If we see a move we can kill em…
02.Alpha TC 25:04 burning building	Miller SOT: "That's where they were all spotted before. Right in that corner."
	V.O. AND FINALLY MORE ARTILLERY…
02.Alpha TC 25:28 Marines at wall	SOT: "I think they're pissed."
02.Alpha TC 25:30 Miller and Marine at wall	Nat. SOT Miller: "I think they're dead…"
02.Alpha TC 27:35 Miller reports to camera	Miller Nat. SOT: "I'm pretty sure anybody in that compound…for our purpose, that was a good day."
02.Alpha TC 37:26 Miller low shot.	
02.Alpha TC 36:45 Dynan looks over Miller's shoulder.	V.O. THE MARINES NOW ARE IN SIGHT OF THE AMIR AGHA VILLAGE AND BAZAAR, THE NUCLEUS OF INSURGENT ACTIVITY.

V.O. BUT BEFORE MOVING IN, ALPHA COMPANY MUST FIRST CLEAR THE SURROUNDING AREA.

Dynan Nat. SOT: "Don't move without a guardian angel…it's going to be a maze in there…avoid bunkers…it's a one-trick pony…we'll get air…"

Miller Nat. SOT: "If it's OK with you we'll throw a grenade in there…"

02.Alpha TC 39:52 Marines push out of compound.

Nat. SOT.

V.O. THE TEMPERATURE RISES TO ABOUT 120 DEGREES.

02.Alpha TC 40:50 shattering glass as Marines move.

Nat. SOT.

02.Alpha TC 41:33 Miller commanding

Miller SOT: "We should leave a team here…"

02.Alpha TC 42:42 Miller

Miller SOT: "Hey what's been cleared on the right side?"

02.Alpha TC 43:50 Marines walk into Dynan frame.

Nat SOT.

02.Alpha TC 48:07 good sequence/noise and Marines back and forth in maze.

V.O. THE MARINES FIND A BUNKER THAT HAD BEEN USED TO AMBUSH ONE OF THEIR PATROLS JUST DAYS BEFORE. ONE MARINE WAS KILLED HERE. THESE MARINES PREPARE TO BLOW IT UP.

02.Alpha TC 58:45 on the radio

"The chem light is on the wall by the bunker…"

02.Alpha TC 46:13 Miller says no resistance

Miller Nat. SOT: "This is a snake of a compound…no resistance…"

02.Alpha TC 44:25 pan across empty courtyard

V.O. NEITHER RESISTANCE – NOR CIVILIANS THE STREETS ARE DESERTED AS THE MARINES CONTINUE THEIR SWEEP.

02.Alpha TC 47:44 pan across empty courtyard
02.Alpha TC 45:37 blows lock off door.

02.Alpha TC 46:48 Dynan and various map. V.O. THERE MAY BE NO RESISTANCE BUT THAT DOESN'T MEAN THERE'S NO DANGER.

02.Alpha TC 49:49 good Miller track Great Nat. SOT. Radios, Marines talking.

02.Alpha TC 50:14 Marines see arty shell Nat. SOT: "Whao. What's that right there? Oh, you mean the fuckin' arty shell that's sitting right there?"

02.Alpha TC 50:43 cu artillery shell

V.O. THE MARINES ARE TOO PRESSED FOR TIME TO DETERMINE WHETHER THIS ARTILLERY ROUND SIMPLY FAILED TO EXPLODE OR WAS WIRED TO KILL THEM.

02.Alpha TC 50:58 Miller orders on machine gun and zoom into Dynan. Great Nat. SOT.

02.Alpha TC 51:29 a very tired and sweaty Miller explains op. Miller SOT.

02.Alpha TC 52:05 two-story bell tower

II. THE MARINES

03.Alpha TC 35:27 Dynan in silhouette Marines set up command post in compound.
V.O. CAPTAIN SEAN DYNAN HAS SET UP A COMMAND POST ON THE EDGE OF THE AMIR AGHA VILLAGE AND BAZAAR.

03.Alpha TC 36:57 cu gun at lookout Nat. SOT TC 37:02 "They're going to be able to see us real good when the sun comes up…and we'll be blinded."

03.Alpha TC 36:18 cu port with light coming in SOT
Nat.

03.Alpha TC 37:23 Marine with gun at port Nat. SOT

03.Alpha TC 36:36 ms Marines looking through port Nat. SOT

03.Alpha TC 07:23 ls at bazaar V.O. THIS SPRAWLING BAZAAR IS THE PRIZE OF THE OPERATION.

04.Alpha TC 18:24 V.O. AND THE MARINES MOVE OUT TO THE

VILLAGE THAT SURROUNDS IT.

04.Alpha TC 20:50 patrol in Amir Agha

V.O. ON THE RIGHT, FIELDS OF WHEAT. ON THE LEFT, FIELDS OF DRIED POPPIES. THIS IS THE YIN AND YANG OF THE AFGHAN FARMERS' EXISTENCE. OPIUM YIELDS MORE PROFIT THAN WHEAT, BUT IT'S ILLEGAL HERE. THE TALIBAN HAS FORCED MANY FARMERS TO CULTIVATE OPIUM SO THEY CAN FINANCE THEIR INSURGENCY.

V.O. THESE POPPIES HAVE BEEN HARVESTED.

01.Alpha TC 31:54, 36:40 cu and ms to zoom and ws poppy field.

V.O. FARMERS MAKE SLASH MARKS ON THE BULBS, WHICH OOZE A GOOEY SAP. THAT SUBSTANCE IS OPIUM.

02.Alpha TC 53:18 hatchet in front of hut

V.O. FIVE YEARS AGO, U.S. POLICY WAS TO DESTROY THESE FIELDS. VILLAGERS WERE ENRAGED. NOW THE MARINES LEAVE THE FIELDS INTACT. THEY NEED THE GOOD WILL OF THE LOCAL POPULATION.

04.Alpha TC 24:20

02.Alpha TC 47:15 plane pix on wall.

V.O. EVERYWHERE THE TROOPS GO, THEY FIND EVIDENCE THAT THE VILLAGERS LEFT IN A TREMENDOUS HURRY.

04.Alpha TC 31:10 Marines shoot then kick in door.

Nat. SOT.

04.Alpha TC 15:21 living room

04.Alpha TC 12:56, 13:01 tea kettle, dishes.

05.Alpha TC 35:52 tea kettle pan to shoe
09.Alpha TC 56:15

V.O. ... LIKE THIS BABY'S CRIB, STILL WITH THE MATTRESS AND BLANKET.

05.Alpha TC 36:43

V.O. ...AND THIS TOOL USED TO COLLECT THE OPIUM FROM POPPY BULBS...

04.Alpha TC 13:13

V.O. BICYCLES, DISHES AND HOUSE WARE, LIKE THIS STRAINER APPARENTLY DONATED BY THE UNITED STATES.

13.Alpha TC tea kettles, dishes, strainer...

V.O. THERE IS A BREAK IN THE FIGHTING

	AND THE MARINES FALL INTO THE ROUTINE OF LIFE IN THE FIELD.
3.Alpha TC 04:53 Miller's guys read Maxim. 06:55 cu magazine. 07:13 ws with Miller in background.	Nat. SOT: "I need to buy one…"
14.Alpha TC 48:26 Marines unload truck.	V.O. IT'S NOW SAFE ENOUGH TO SEND A TRUCKLOAD OF SUPPLIES TO DYNAN'S FORWARD COMMAND POST, INCLUDING MUCH NEEDED WATER, FOR THE 200 MARINES IN ALPHA COMPANY.
13.Alpha 59:13 Marines play cards.	
17.Alpha TC 25:45 Marines wash helmets.	V.O. THEY ARE AMONG THE TOUGHEST OF THE AMERICAN MILITARY. THERE'S A MYSTIQUE ABOUT THE MARINES, A TRADITION OF ACHIEVING MORE WITH LESS AND TAKING ON THE MOST DANGEROUS ADVERSARIES.
17.Alpha TC 25:00 Marines dig burn pit. 17.Alpha TC 26:07 digging. 17.Alpha TC 26:50 "What you digging?	Nat. SOT
08.Alpha TC 33:21 promotion ceremony	V.O. TODAY CAPTAIN DYNAN PROMOTES ONE OF HIS MEN IN A CEREMONY RIGHT ON THE BATTLEFIELD.
05.Alpha TC 07:46 long pan of Marines asleep in compound.	
05.Alpha TC 48:00 Marines asleep in compound.	V.O. THESE MEN HAVE BECOME FAMILY, BONDED BY ONE OF THE MOST FORMATIVE EXPERIENCES OF THEIR YOUNG LIVES.
07.Alpha TC 23:55 Marines sing Amazing Grace.	
FADE TO BLACK.	

III. THE BAZAAR

08.Alpha TC 59:54	V.O. IN EARLY MORNING LIGHT I MOVE OUT WITH 4TH PLATOON TO CLEAR THE BAZAAR. IT'S THE LAST STEP OF THE MILITARY OPERATION BEFORE THEY CAN START MAKING PEACE.

	V.O. AND IT COULD BE THE MOST DANGEROUS. THE TALIBAN HAVE CONTROLLED THIS BAZAAR FOR TWO YEARS AND THEY'VE HAD PLENTY OF TIME TO SET UP DEFENSIVE POSITIONS, AND TO WIRE IT WITH TRAPS AND EXPLOSIVES.
08.Alpha TC 00:03 Marines to bazaar	Nat. SOT.
08.Alpha TC 00:33 cross puddle	Nat. SOT.
08.Alpha TC 00:43 tense Marine	
08.Alpha TC 01:31 chopper	V.O. THE MARINES ARE COVERED BY ATTACK HELICOPTERS.
08.Alpha TC 01:51	V.O. THE STREETS ARE EMPTY. AND IT'S SLOW GOING.
08.Alpha TC 03:55 metal detector	V.O. ONE MARINE USES A METAL DETECTOR FOR IMPROVISED EXPLOSIVE DEVICES, OR IEDs THAT ARE SO INFAMOUS AND SO DEADLY IN IRAQ. NOW INSURGENTS ARE USING THEM HERE.
08.Alpha TC 05:05 Marine covers detector	Nat. SOT.
	V.O. THE MARINES MOVE DOOR TO DOOR BLOWING THE LOCKS OFF THE STALLS.
08.Alpha TC 13:40 Dynan turns to see Marines opening stall door Blowing locks	V.O. CAPTAIN DYNAN OVERSEES THE OPERATION.

V.O. FOR SEAN DYNAN, COMMANDING A COMPANY OF MARINES IS A DREAM COME TRUE.DYNAN IS FOURTH GENERATION MILITARY OF HIS IRISH FAMILY, WHICH CLAIMS FOUR PURPLE HEARTS SINCE WORLD WAR TWO.

V.O. HE WAS RAISED JUST OUTSIDE OF BOSTON AND GRADUATED FROM THE U.S. NAVAL ACADEMY AT ANNAPOLIS, MARYLAND. DYNAN'S BEEN A MARINE FOR TEN YEARS.

V.O. THIS IS HIS FOURTH DEPLOYMENT, THE MOST RECENT IN RAMADI, IRAQ, SO HE KNOWS SOMETHING ABOUT ROUGH NEIGHBORHOODS.

Marines on bazaar street.
Treptow to camera

Nat SOT: "It may be something…"

08.Alpha TC 19:37 flag pan to freezer & ws

V.O. LIEUTENANT JACK TREPTOW AND 4TH PLATOON COME ACROSS A PADLOCKED FREEZER. HE SUSPECTS THE RED FLAG JUST ACROSS THE STREET SIGNIFIES A TRAP.

V.O. LIKE DYNAN, TREPTOW AND MANY OF THESE MARINES ALREADY HAVE SERVED IN IRAQ AND THEY KNOW HOW DEADLY THESE INNOCENT-LOOKING THINGS CAN BE.

08.Alpha TC 09:36 sweeper and boom.

Nat. SOT

08.Alpha TC 17:07 Lt. Treptow on radio

Nat. SOT: "We have an industrial size refrigerator…"

08.Alpha TC 19:03

08.Alpha TC 21:20 bomb squad rolls up and Treptow talks with Sam

09.Alpha TC 22:09 Sam walks up followed by Humvee

09.Alpha TC 27:19 robot on the move.

V.O. THEY USE A REMOTE-CONTROLLED ROBOT TO EXAMINE THE FREEZER CLOSE-

	UP, AND EXPOSIVES TO BLOW THE LOCK AND CHAIN OFF THE FREEZER DOOR.

09.Alpha TC 28:45 Sam watches robot then speaks to camera.
09.Alpha TC 31:30 Sam checks out fridge, cuts wires & returns to report.
09.Alpha TC 33:35 Sam returns & Treptow radios.
09.Alpha TC 34:59 light fuse

09.Alpha TC 35:19 blow
09.Alpha TC 35:50 run up & see soda.   Nat SOT: "Nope. Harmless."
09.Alpha TC 47:41 bang locks & enter

08.Alpha TC 07:50 cu frontal Marine covers   Nat. SOT
08.Alpha TC 08:05 ms from other side.
(intercut with mine sweeper.)   V.O. THIS TIME, IT'S ONLY SOFT DRINKS.

09.Alpha TC 50:43 shotgun blast & door up.
09.Alpha TC 52:27 another shotgun blast & door open.
09.Alpha TC 53:23 Cobra sweeps bazaar.
TC Marines walk through poppy fields.
09.Alpha TC 57:39 Marines share smokes.

09.Alpha TC 02:00 Marines on smoke break.   V.O. THE PLATOON TAKES A SMOKE BREAK AND LT. TREPTOW BRINGS THEM UP TO DATE.

09.Alpha TC 58:30 Treptow informs Marines.   Treptow Nat. SOT: "…We're going to find a ton of s… during this sweep…"
10.Alpha TC 26:02   V.O. AND IT DID: MORTARS ALREADY WIRED AS ROADSIDE BOMBS.

10.Alpha TC 25:35 RPGs   V.O. ROCKET PROPELLED GRENADES.

10.Alpha TC 27:08 ammunition.
10.Alpha TC 26:53   V.O. AMMUNITION AND WEAPONS.
Nat. SOT: "…bayonets…"

10.Alpha TC 21:15 4th Platoon rests   V.O. THE BAZAAR IS CLEAR. THE
against wall.   COMBAT PART OF THE MISSION HAS BEEN ACCOMPLISHED.

IV. CLEAR, HOLD, BUILD

V.O. BUT WHAT COMES NEXT IS JUST AS TOUGH. THE MARINES NEED TO WIN THE TRUST OF THE LOCALS WHO HAVE BEEN LIVING IN A BATTLE ZONE FOR YEARS.

06.Alpha TC 18:44 pan Humvee
window to driver.

06.Alpha TC 19:30 peasant passes
Humvee window.
06.Alpha TC 19:51 thru windshield.

06.Alpha TC 21:20 boy and woman on
roadside as Humvee passes.

06.Alpha TC 23:25 terp and CA Marine
approach locals

V.O. THEY REACH OUT TO CIVILIANS WHO
HAD TAKEN REFUGE IN THE NEARBY
DESERT. STILL WARRIORS, THE MARINES
NOW ARE DIPLOMATS.

V.O. EXILED DURING THE FIGHTING, THE
CIVILIANS ARE EAGER TO RETURN HOME.

Nat. SOT: "Salam Alaikum…how are you
today?"

06.Alpha TC 32:28

V.O. BUT NOT ALL THE CIVILIANS ARE
HAPPY. SAID GUL TELLS THE MARINES HIS
HOME HAS BEED DAMAGED BY AMERICAN
BOMBS AND ARTILLERY.

07.Alpha TC 34:10 great side cu Said.

07.Alpha TC 35:10 cu Said son pan up.

07.Alpha TC 44:48 great ms man sitting

with donkey passing in background.	Nat. SOT
07.Alpha TC 45:30 Said urging them to visit his home.	V.O. SAID URGES THE MARINES TO COME TO HIS HOME TO SEE THE DAMAGE -- AND ASKS THEM TO PAY FOR IT.
07.Alpha TC 49:40 loaded camel past Humvee.	
06.Alpha ms more locals with Marines	V.O. ALL OF THESE MEN WANT SOMETHING. V.O. THIS MAN SAYS A WOUND ON HIS SON'S CHEST IS INFECTED AND THE BOY NEEDS HELP. V.O. OTHERS ASK THE MARINES FOR HELP WITH IRRIGATION.
06.Alpha TC 26:25 Terp talking to locals	Terp SOT: "They want to go turn their pumps on."
06.Alpha TC 30:47	Terp and Juan SOT: "How many gallons of fuel we can give him?...Tell him eight."
07.Alpha TC 53:45 Humvees along canal	V.O. THE MARINES DECIDE TO HAND OVER DIESEL, WHICH FUELS THE WATER PUMPS. V.O. THE MEN SAID THEY HAD NOT USED THE PUMPS – AND THEIR CROPS HAD NOT BEEN WATERED – DURING THE PAST 40 DAYS BECAUSE THEY HAD EVACUATED THE AREA.
07.Alpha TC 04:00 engine starts	Nat. SOT on boom microphone.
07.Alpha TC 55:33	V.O. SAID GUL IS HERE TO PRESS HIS CASE FOR HELP. HE IS A RESPECTED LAND OWNER HERE -- 38 YEARS OLD, MARRIED WITH 12 CHILDREN.
07.Alpha TC 55:45	V.O. HE SAYS HIS HOUSE IS JUST ACROSS THE CANAL. HE CULTIVATES WHEAT AND POPPIES, AND HAS A SMALL CLOTHING SHOP IN THE BAZAAR. V.O. HE OFFERS UP THIS BAG OF OPIUM IN RETURN FOR HELP. V.O. THE MARINES DECLINE HIS OFFER.

07.Alpha TC 08:49

Terp SOT: "All six rooms have collapsed…"

V.O. SAID IS NOT OPTIMISTIC THAT HE WILL GET HELP. AND HIS WORDS INDICATE HOW DIFFICULT THE MARINES' MISSION WILL BE. A CIVILIAN INTERPRETER TRANSLATES HIS COMMENTS:

07.Alpha TC Said Gul interview

Said Gul Nat. SOT: "Americans came here telling us they are going to help us, they are going to build things, but these are tricks, the same tricks that the Russians played. They said they came here as friends telling us they are going to help us but then they started killing us, martyring people so we don't trust the foreigners anymore.

V.O. SAID GUL SPEAKS FOR MANY OF THE VILLAGERS CAUGHT IN THE MIDDLE OF A WAR THAT NEVER SEEMS TO END.

"We are the people in the middle. What we do is just follow the religion of Islam. We're just simple workers. We just want to go on with our lives."

V.O. ALPHA COMPANY'S COMPOUND IS NOW A SMALL FORTRESS, PROTECTED AGAINST ATTACK AND SUICIDE BOMBERS.

14.Alpha TC 22:44

14.Alpha TC 22:22

14.Alpha TC 23:30

V.O. FOUR DAYS AFTER OUR ENCOUNTER AT THE CANAL, SAID GUL MEETS AT THE COMMAND POST WITH CIVIL AFFAIRS OFFICERS. HE WANTS MONEY FOR THE DAMAGE TO HIS HOME.

14.Alpha TC 26:10 Said looks nervous.

14.Alpha TC 26:40 Dynan comes in and looks at map, confirms site of home and firefight.

Dynan Nat. SOT.

28:08 two-shot as Bechtel strokes chin

14.Alpha TC 30:55 cu Said

Terp SOT: "He said he put a lot of money

	into that house.." and CA, "Well what would it cost to rebuild?"
14.Alpha TC 33:47 ws	CA SOT: "Very well, tell him I don't have the money right now…"
14.Alpha TC 40:13 USE AS CUTAWAY?	
14.Alpha TC 40:50 cu "do not enter"	
14.Alpha TC 44:06 Said shakes hands, leaves.	V.O. SAID GUL WON'T GET ANY MONEY TODAY.
	V.O. THE MARINES MUST WIN THE TRUST OF THE VILLAGERS BUT THEY MUST ALSO OVERCOME THEIR FEAR.
10. Alpha TC 30:44 Marines find the dead guy	V.O. THESE VILLAGERS LEAD THE MARINES TO A DEAD MAN WHOSE THROAT WAS SLIT, THEY SAID, BY THE TALIBAN. THEY SAY IT'S A WARNING NOT TO COOPERATE WITH THE AMERICANS.
10.Alpha TC 31:10 villagers walking.	V.O. THEY BURIED HIM WHERE THEY FOUND HIM.
10.Alpha TC 32:30 cu dead man. 10.Alpha TC 33:45 villagers dig grave.	

10.Alpha TC 36:00 Dynan giving night-time speech.	V.O. THAT SAME NIGHT, CAPTAIN DYNAN COACHES HIS MARINES ON HOW THEIR MISSION HAS CHANGED.
LARRY, SEE TAPE #3, AT TC 34:00 FOR LOTS OF SILHOUETTES THAT MIGHT BE USEABLE HERE.	
10.Alpha TC 35:15	Dynan Nat. SOT: "In the last 48 hours our mission has changed significantly…gone from taking fire to locals flooding the area…
10.Alpha TC 35:54	
	V.O. IT'S A DIFFERENT KIND OF BATTLE NOW.
10.Alpha TC 36:14	… and it will be a little tougher now…you treating a human being like a human being is going to make a huge difference…
10.Alpha TC 35:14	

FADE TO BLACK

Dynan standing in line meeting villagers	V.O. DYNAN HOSTS A SHURRA, OR MEETING OF LOCAL ELDERS. HE UNDERSTANDS THE IMPORTANCE OF THESE TRADITIONAL GATHERINGS. AND HE WANTS TO FORGE TIES WITH THE LOCALS AS SOON AS POSSIBLE.
	V.O. BECAUSE THIS AREA WAS OCCUPIED BY THE TALIBAN, THIS IS THE FIRST SHURRA THESE MEN HAVE ATTENDED IN THREE YEARS.
15.Alpha TC 07:49 man comes up to entrance for shurra.	Dynan Nat. SOT: "Sallam…"
15.Alpha TC 08:04 man approaches,	Dynan Nat. SOT: "When we throw a party we
Dynan on attendance.	go all out.."
15.Alpha TC 08:40 Dynan repeatedly …	Dynan Nat. SOT: "Sallam…"
15.Alpha TC 09:24 shakes hands.	
15.Alpha TC 09:50 guy snags on wire.	Dynan Nat. SOT: "Oh jeez…"
15.Alpha TC 10:39 through wire.	

Various men seated at shurra.

V.O. THIS IS WHAT THE MARINES CALL "THE CENTER OF GRAVITY." THESE ARE THE HEARTS AND MINDS THAT MUST BE WON TO DEFEAT THE TALIBAN. THE MARINES DESCRIBE THEIR STRATEGY AS CLEAR, HOLD AND BUILD. BUT WITHOUT THE SUPPORT OF THE VILLAGERS THERE CAN BE NO "HOLD." AND THERE CAN BE NO "BUILD."

15.Alpha TC 21:46

V.O. IN ATTENDANCE ARE THE DISTRICT GOVERNOR AND THE CHIEF OF POLICE...

15.Alpha TC 38:15 Said Gul in crowd.

V.O. ...AND NOT SURPRISINGLY, SAID GUL.

15.Alpha TC 15:32 Dynan addresses shurra

Dynan Nat. SOT: "I am honored to be sitting amongst you right now...I know we are just another face after 30 years of people coming through this area...we must answer how we are different... you don't want us to interfere...It is our intention to help and to protect you.

V. EPILOGUE

16.Alpha TC 00:07 little girl in doorway

V.O. THE DAY AFTER THE SHURRA, CIVILIANS RETURN EN MASSE TO THEIR HOMES AND THEIR LIVELIHOODS.

16.Alpha TC 00:59 GREAT shot peasant in poppy field.

16.Alpha TC 00:05 two guys on bike, end at Dynan.

16.Alpha TC 17:11 old man on bike, sheep. USE.

Nat. SOT.
V.O. SHEPARDS RETURN WITH THEIR LIVESTOCK TO THE CANALS.

16.Alpha TC 38:00
16.Alpha TC 38:10
16.Alpha TC 28:48
16.Alpha TC 29:10

V.O. SHOP OWNERS RETURN TO THE BAZAAR. AND THE POLICE RE-ESTABLISH A PRESENCE FOR THE FIRST TIME IN TWO YEARS.

16.Alpha TC 37:25

V.O. AND YOU KNOW THINGS HAVE
CHANGED WHEN THE KIDS SHOW UP.
I GIVE THESE LITTLE GUYS A LOOK AT
THEMSELVES THROUGH MY CAMERA'S
VIEWING SCREEN.

V.O. IT'S PEACEFUL HERE NOW, BUT
DYNAN UNDERSTANDS THAT THIS IS
MERELY THE END OF THE BEGINNING.

18.Alpha TC 44:40 Marines cross log
on canal.

V.O. DURING THE LAST DAYS OF MY
EMBED, CAPTAIN DYNAN TOOK ME TO
SAID GUL'S COMPOUND.

V.O. THAT'S IT, IN THE BACKGROUND.

18.Alpha TC 45:00

"Wait for them to come to us. You have to
be invited in."

V.O. IT'S SURROUNDED BY POPPIES AND
MARIJUANA PLANTS. SAID APPARENTLY
HAS BEEN NAPPING. EVEN THE LOCALS
HAVE TROUBLE WITH THE AFTERNOON
HEAT.

V.O. DYNAN GETS A FIRST-HAND LOOK AT
DAMAGE CAUSED TO SAID GUL'S HOUSE
DURING THE MARINES' BATTLES WITH THE
TALIBAN.

18.Alpha TC 46:40

"I understand there was some damage to
your compound?"

18.Alpha TC 49:10

Dynan SOT: "Any information on Taliban?"

V.O. ABOUT A MONTH AFTER THIS
ENCOUNTER, I GOT WORD THAT THE
MARINES HAD PAID SAID GUL HALF THE
MONEY HE WANTED TO REPAIR HIS HOME.
AND THE REST WAS ON ITS WAY.

16.Alpha TC 03:08 Marines walk away
from camera, Humvees passing.

V.O. THESE MARINES MAY YET WIN OVER
SAID GUL AND THE OTHER LOCALS HERE.
BUT THERE HAVE BEEN SETBACKS IN
OTHER PARTS OF THE COUNTRY.

****IS THERE TAPE OF THIS OR PIX*

V.O. JUST THIS WEEK, TALIBAN REBELS NEARLY OVERRAN A U.S. MILITARY OUTPOST IN KUNAR PROVINCE, KILLING NINE AMERICAN SERVICEMEN AND FORCING OTHERS TO RETREAT.

24 May #1 TC 07:37 Marines in dust storm in

FOB Dwyer.

[[need SOT from Dynan or other commander
to break this up]]

V.O. THE PENTAGON AGREES ON THE NEED FOR MORE TROOPS HERE.

V.O. IN FACT, EARLIER THIS YEAR THE MARINE CORPS PROPOSED TO MAKE AFGHANISTAN, NOT IRAQ, ITS PRIMARY MISSION. THE DEFENSE DEPARTMENT SAID NO, AND HAS DECIDED THAT NEW TROOPS CAN'T BE SENT HERE UNTIL MORE ARE WITHDRAWN FROM IRAQ.

17.Alpha TC 30:14 Marines file out of doorway to patrol.

V.O. THE 24TH MARINE EXPEDITIONARY UNIT HAS MAKE HEADWAY IN THIS VALLEY... BUT TO EXPAND THESE EFFORTS ACROSS AFGHANISTAN WILL BE A MAJOR CHALLENGE FOR AMERICA'S NEXT PRESIDENT.

V.O. AS FOR THESE MARINES, THEIR TOUR OF DUTY HAS JUST BEEN EXTENDED UNTIL NOVEMBER.

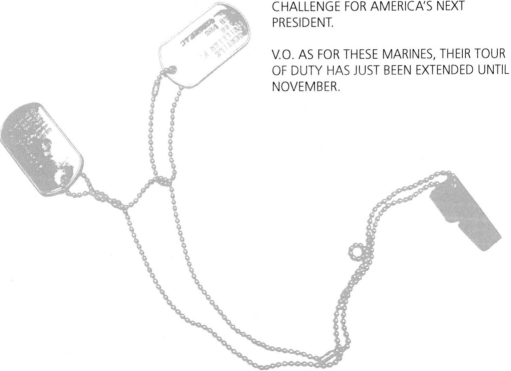

We began this manual with me telling you about how journalism has been my ticket and my tool, and how I've managed to keep pace with the technology that has so drastically impacted how we practice the craft. We started with some of the black-and-white pictures I made during the 1979 Sandinista Revolution in Nicaragua. In this picture, it's 2008 and I'm editing a high-definition, 23-minute documentary piece I did from Afghanistan on the 24th Marine Expeditionary Unit (24thMEU) in the Helmand River Valley along the border with Pakistan. That's how far and how fast we've come just in the time I've been practicing the craft.

Treatment • FRONTLINE JOURNALISTS

NOTE: Following is <u>only part</u> of the treatment I wrote for a documentary I shot in 2005 about the foreign correspondents working in Afghanistan. The entire treatment is very long, and I didn't want to burn up too much space. I include this small portion to give you a sense of how "visual" the treatment should be, much like the proposal.

FRONTLINE JOURNALISTS:
Death and Danger in Afghanistan
a film
by
Bill Gentile

I. Introduction

We hear the rumble of a Chinook transport helicopter. The noise grows louder. We see the rotor, the machine gun pointing at the jagged mountains outside the door. We see the gunner, the cockpit and pilots.

Then the screen goes to silent black and we hear Andrew North of the BBC report on the downing of the helicopter as it attempted to pick up four U.S. Navy SEALs caught in a running gun battle with Taliban guerrillas in Afghanistan's Kunar Province. We see Andrew's picture on the television screen.

The BBC's Andrew North is the only foreign correspondent close to what would become the single most deadly incident in the history of the SEALs, the elite of America's fighting units. North is embedded with U.S. troops at a base in the region when the Arab television outlet, Al Jazeera, reports that Taliban guerrillas have shot down the craft.

Details of the incident are slow to emerge. What is known is that 16 American servicemen in the helicopter are killed in the crash. One member of the four-man SEAL team has been rescued but the other three are missing. The gun battle and subsequent helicopter crash occurred in a remote area of Afghanistan's Kunar Province. But the area, crawling with Taliban guerrillas, is accessible only on foot or by helicopter. And none of the other correspondents based in the region is so lucky as the BBC's North, who happens to be on an American military base at the time of the incident.

We see Carlotta Gall of The New York Times in her Kabul office, with one of her two assistants. She is on the phone with National Public Radio in Washington, DC.

"We don't know much except one Navy SEAL was picked up," Gall says into the phone. "We've heard he's in good health and he's been able to talk and pass on information about his five days that he was in the mountains – evading the Taliban. There's still no news of the other three."

Even the correspondent for what is arguably the world's most important newspaper can't get to the bottom of the story and must rely on the reports of her BBC colleague.

"I'm taking that from the BBC," Gall continues. "There's a BBC correspondent on one of the US bases in eastern Afghanistan."

Marketing: Getting Your Work Noticed
Marketing Yourself and Your Work

I've been asked about how one translates the skills you are learning into real income that you generate out in the field. This is an important question that anyone considering work as a freelance journalist should be asking him/herself.

And it is for this reason that I've asked J. Bruce Jones to contribute a special section on marketing for this new edition of the Field Manual. This is Bruce's specialty. We've been working together since 2008 when he first attended one of my Video Journalism Workshops in Washington, DC. He's an Internet marketer with dozens of books under his belt, and understands how to sell one's work online more than anyone I know. So while I provide a brief overview here, please see Bruce's section that begins on page 155.

The answer to the question about how to market yourself and your work is multi-faceted. And some of you already know many of the answers. The key to your successful economic model, I believe, is diversity.

What you are doing now is building a commodity – yourself. Your task in general is to incorporate all the knowledge and skills into this commodity so you can walk into the market and say, "Buy me."

And the term "Me" is partly defined by what you are able to present to people on the Internet. So, if you do not already have a web site, your first priority is to get one. Nobody hands out paper resumes anymore. If you can't be found on the Internet with a Google search, then for many "buyers" you do not exist. So get the site up, with your resume and samples of your work. It's the quickest way employers can find out who you are. Take a look at mine, www.billgentile.com. Nothing fancy, but you get the point.

Build your social network. Start by setting up a Facebook page. Then get a Twitter account. Then build a LinkedIn account.

Now set up a blog. Learn to use the tags and the language in the body and headlines of your blog posts to drive traffic to your web site, which is your online advertisement. This really is an art, a craft unto itself. And there are people who know far more about this than I, so I won't even go down this road right now. But if you work this strategy long and hard enough, your name can become synonymous with your craft, or at least your very own slice of the craft. Google the term "backpack journalism," for example, and you'll see me come up on the first page. This is not an accident. This is the result of me driving traffic to my site and my blog through the social networking tools I mention above. It's the result of me defining myself and my work, and driving traffic to my online presence.

Once you've produced some work you want associated with your name, set up a Vimeo channel, which is a much cleaner platform for your work than is YouTube. Check out my Vimeo channel, "Backpack Journalist."

Now set up a YouTube channel.

Sign up to www.withoutabox.com. This is a key tool for anybody who wants to stay informed about what is happening in the world of independent documentary production. This will provide you with the latest information regarding the more than 500 independent film festivals in this country (and others overseas) and how you fit in. You will create a profile for yourself and your work. It's a great resource.

OK. So you've identified yourself. You're connected. You're informed. How do you actually make money? And where? How do you fund your projects?

It is no secret that the television market for the kind of production that many of us want to do is shrinking. The Internet market, on the other hand, is expanding, and the online components of existing outlets are a potential market for our work.

Perhaps more importantly, private businesses, NGOs, non-profits and government all are increasingly conscious that communication is increasingly visual. And video is a key component of that communication. Almost irrespective of the field, video plays an increasingly important role in it. For those who can speak the visual language, the opportunities are limitless.

Gaining access to these outlets is a question of contacting those responsible for content. And the key to selling your work to any of these conventional outlets is to make connections with editors BEFORE you head out the door for a project. Though you may have constructed the above-mentioned social network, nothing takes the place of a face-to-face meeting with the editor who will be accepting or rejecting your work once you are in the field.

There is also an emerging online market that aspires to compete with the online components of conventional media outlets.

For example, I signed a freelance contract with VJ Movement, an Internet outlet based in The Netherlands. It works as a cooperative and pays decent money for a

3-5 minute video piece. See http://www.vjmovement.com. Perhaps it is not a tremendous amount of money but an association with this group can be one component of your multifaceted economic model. Again, it's about diversity.

As we already have discussed, mainstream American media have contracted their operations, particularly overseas. Into this void are stepping a number of organizations whose managers understand the critical role of independent media.

For example, as a professor at American University, I've worked quite a bit with the Pulitzer Center on Crisis Reporting, which provides grants to applicants aspiring to report on important stories overseas. See http://www.pulitzercenter.org.

The Pulitzer Center's efforts are similar to those of the International Reporting Project (IRP) in that both sponsor journalists who want to cover important issues abroad. And both promote those journalists' work upon their return to the United States. See http://www.internationalreportingproject.org.

Check out both of these organizations, which can fund and promote your work.

This overview is, simply put, an overview. Please refer to the new, special section on marketing by J. Bruce Jones, for a much more detailed discussion of this topic. It begins on page 155.

IV.
Resources

Resources: Following are some resources you may find useful.

Personal Gear List

Below is a list of items you might consider for journeys to out-of-the-way locations. These are only suggestions. They are not in any particular order.

First and foremost are the tools you will need to execute your work: Your camera gear and computer. Please review your gear before hitting the road. Test it today. Make sure you are capturing quality images and sound. Make sure you have the necessary cables to move those images and sound through your computer to an external hard drive. Make sure you know how to transfer that material into your video editing program. Please don't forget the earphones (I use the kind you plug into your ears) not just for your shoots but also for editing. These will enable you to edit your piece without bothering your neighbors with the sound.

You may need a backpack to carry your gear from the hotel to the field. Although you may carry your camera in your hand for that brief trip, you probably will want some kind of backpack to carry wireless microphones, batteries, tape, water, sun block, and other items.

Hard case with a lock. I generally use one to safeguard my equipment when I leave it in a hotel room. A good lock is essential. Especially in poor countries, I try not to tempt hotel workers by leaving unguarded any of the cool stuff that I bring into the country.

Of course you will need a current passport. Bring any medicines that you take regularly.

Footwear. This is very, very important. You might want to bring a decent pair of sandals for time off around the pool or lounging at the hotel, but a good, solid pair of work shoes, like hiking boots with ankle support, will protect your feet from injury, disease, broken glass, nails, etc. And get some decent socks, preferably wool, or "Smart Wool" as it is called, to repel moisture away from your skin. Cotton socks will absorb moisture, keep your feet wet all day and complicate your life with painful blisters.

Hat. Get a good hat with a brim to keep the sun from pounding you into submission during the day.

Sun block. Another key item on this list.

Mosquito repellant. A good thing to have in the evening while working or if we step out to dinner. I find the Coleman "botanicals" with lemon eucalyptus oil to be very effective and non-toxic, as it doesn't contain DEET.

Swiss Army Knife (Explorer model). Chances are you won't need one but when you do, it's great to have.

Pens. Take a couple of different kinds, including fine-tipped permanent pens.

Reporter's Notebooks. Critical not only for taking notes but also for jotting down ideas on whatever story you are covering.

Gaffer's tape. NOT duct tape, which leaves a residue on everything it touches. Gaffer's tape is one of the visual journalist's best friends.

Rain poncho. Especially useful during the rainy season.

Chamois. Get a real one (not cloth) at an auto supply store. They are big, like 12 inches X 12 inches or so. Can be extremely handy keeping gear dry during the rainy season and wiping lenses dry.

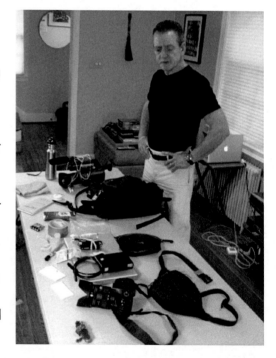

Head lamp. If you work at night this can be very useful for handling your gear or just walking from one place to the next in places where there are no street lights. I recommend the small but powerful Petzl models that strap to your head, thereby allowing both hands to stay free.

Dust brush. Get a little paint brush with a soft tip at a hardware store. Like the chamois, its good for cleaning lenses and gear.

Three-prong to two-pronged electrical adapters. The wall outlets in some countries are two-pronged versions and you will need an adaptor to plug in your gear.

Wet Wipes. These are very useful in the field to clean your hands and face before and after meals. They also can be extremely useful as a substitute for toilet paper in places where there very often is none.

Water container. You want to bring your own refillable water container.

Belly pack. I always use one of these, in which I keep a chamois, a brush, batteries, earphones and earplugs, Wet Wipes, etc.

Sunglasses. Protect your eyes. You only have two of them.

Pants with pockets/shirts with long sleeves. Jeans are OK but they can be heavy and hot. If you get them wet, they stay that way all day long. And at night-time, mosquitoes love to attack dark colors (and your legs). So I use khaki-colored pants that dry in minutes if you get them wet and, because of the light color, don't attract mosquitoes. Some have pockets, which is a bonus. I also use moisture-re-pelling undershirts made of 100 percent polyester under khaki-colored, long-sleeve shirts that repel UV rays. All this stuff is available at outdoor stores like REI.

Ziplock bags. I use the large version of these bags to store lenses, wireless micro-phones, batteries, hard drives and anything else that could be harmed by dust or moisture.

You may want to bring a swimsuit for down time at the pool or the beach. And I probably will bring a yoga mat to unwind after long hours in the field.

Other Resources
For a comprehensive list of other resources you may find useful, please review my Foreign Correspondence blog that I maintain for my class of the same name at

American University. You can find it here: https://foreigncorrespondencenet.word-press.com/resourses-combined/

Bill Gentile's "Wait! Don't Shoot!" Tips

Wait! Don't Shoot! Not, at least, until you review this check list!

Even professional video journalists with many years of field experience sometimes forget to review the basics before picking up the camera to shoot. Run through this list each time before you shoot so you won't have regrets when you're done shooting.

1. Check the focus for "automatic" or "manual," whichever you prefer.
2. Check the iris and shutter speed settings for proper exposure.
3. Check the "gain" switch for the appropriate setting.
4. Make sure you are getting two independent channels of sound. And wear those earplug headphones!!! Always!!!
5. Check the levels of sound.
6. Check the "white balance."
7. Make sure the settings on resolution, frames per second and format are what you want, and that they are consistent with material already shot for the same project. Is it 1080/30p and shutter speed of 50/second? Is it 16 X 9?
8. Make sure you have batteries to power the camera and the wireless microphones. Always power the wireless microphones with new batteries at the beginning of each day. Batteries are cheap. The cost of lost sound can be incalculable.
9. Make sure you have extra tapes or memory cards ready to switch out quickly in case you run out of tape or memory space in the middle of an important shoot.
10. Clean the lens! Clean the lens! Clean the lens!

NOTE: Some of you may want to participate in my Video Journalism Workshops. Below is a compressed schedule of that four-day immersion in the craft of video storytelling.

Schedule: Video Journalism Workshop

Day 1:

- Introductions and objectives.
- Definition of Backpack Journalism/Backpack Documentary.
- View "Chain Gang" as a teaching/training model.
- Clips to Sequence to Scene to Story – the final objective.
- Basic elements of a new language: XCU to XWA.
- The Six-Shot System: Demonstration.
- Composition: The deliberate arrangement of elements in your images.
- The Rule of Thirds and Multiple Planes.
- Gentile's Shooting Rules.
- First shoot: Characters and The Sequence. Casting a wide net.
- Review footage.
- Proposals, Titles and The Controlling Idea.
- View "Echoes of War" and two models of "character-driven" documentaries.

Day 2:

- Present Title and Controlling Idea.
- Opening scene. Closing scene.
- Production Schedule.
- Dramatic Arc.
- View "Voice of Hope" as example of multiple dramatic arcs.
- "Participatory Observation:" Engage your subjects.
- Formal and Informal interviews.
- Gentile's Interview Rules.
- Second shoot:
- Review footage.
- Editing.
- Scripts and Treatments.
- Sound: Heartbeat of Documentary.

Day 3:

- More Titles and Controlling Ideas.
- Marketing Your Work:
- View "Nurses Needed" and discuss characters that embody editorial points.
- Third shoot: Only if necessary.
- Editing and "the creative treatment of reality."
- View "Underground Yoga" and "Knife and Gun Club" as editing models.
- Aesthetics vs. mechanics.
- The script: Writing to pictures.
- Narration, the third dimension of "three-dimensional chess."

Day 4:

- View "Afghanistan: The Forgotten War," as model for narration and storytelling.
- Your conversation with the audience.
- More editing.
- Workshop evaluations.
- View final products.
- Uploading your work to the Internet.

V.

Marketing
YOUR VIDEOS ___
AND YOU
You have made your video, now what?

By J. Bruce Jones

You've made your video, now what? That is the key question that we'll be talking about in this bonus chapter. What happens after you have made your video. How do you get it out to the world? How do you get people to see it? How do you build a presence on-line and how do you even make money out of it? Let's start first with what is the purpose of making videos.

Purposes for Making Videos
You're a documentary filmmaker or you're making videos for an organization or for news or just to tell your story. Video can also be for informing people about your cause or your mission. Video is also used to promote and sell a product. And finally to build your presence in the market or advance your career.

J. Bruce Jones is a 30 year Boston based international best selling author, business graphic designer and consultant. Bruce is the author and creator of over 40 books on music, geography, publishing, coloring and childrens, with several books on the bestseller list. He speaks and consults on publishing, social media, blogging and producing online video. Bruce has been selling products online since 1996.

Bruce Jones attended the very first Video Journalism Workshop with Bill Gentile in Washington DC in 2008. Bruce has since produced hundreds of videos for public access programing and himself. Over the years Bruce has partnered with Bill in a variety of ways and currrently teaches the social media portion of the live workshops.

Marketing Your Videos and You

Build Market Awareness by Building Your Platform

One of the key ways to start building awareness of your videos and to get your message out there, is to start by building a platform. In publishing, a platform is all the places and ways that people connect with you and is a key part of selling books. The same thing happens with promoting, marketing and selling your video content. You need to start getting the world connected to you and building your platform.

Your platform is made up of your e-mail list, your social media followers such as on Facebook, Twitter, and YouTube. These are the people who follow you in any and every way. They are the people who come to your events and who buy your products.

One of the best ways to build an effective platform is to create an e-mail list. To build a list you must have people register on your website using an e-mail sign up box. Generally we will give away some free content as a thank you for signing up. This could be PDF of a chapter of a new book or maybe a resource list or some behind the scenes videos from your latest project. E-mail companies like AWeber and MailChimp are great for doing this and have lots of tools to help you. Building an e-mail list is one of the most important ways of staying connected with people and letting them know what you're doing and also later on to sell them content.

We can also build followers through our social media platforms such as Facebook, Twitter, Linkedin and Pinterest. While not as powerful as an e-mail list it's just as important. Social media is also a very easy way to spread new content and information to your followers.

The key is for you to be in the same places as your audience, where they hang out, you hang out. If they are on Facebook, Twitter, YouTube, or Linkedin then you are also. It is all about engagement and connection.

If you speak publicly, lecture, do appearances, or trainings, these are all great places to connect with people. These are all the people who later on will become your fans, to see your films or buy your products. Be sure to collect names and e-mail addresses.

Build your professional online resume using services like Linkedin. From Google's point of view, Linkedin is one of the best places to learn about a

Marketing Your Videos and You

person. Make sure yours is up-to-date. Don't forget every other social media site has a profile page. Are yours filled out and are they up-to-date? Do you have an About page?

You want to figure out who your audience is, be where they are, then build your platform from that. You don't have to be on every site. If your audience is primarily in Facebook, then you need to be in Facebook. If it's YouTube, be in YouTube.

Connect with the Top 20 Influencers in Your Market

A key strategy to do this, is to identify and connect with the Top 20 or so influencers in your market. Who are they and where do they hang out? Search Google, magazines, bookstores, your industry and related areas. Are they on YouTube? Are they on Twitter? Do they have a blog, a book, a course? Look at their bios, look at their connections.

You want to be in the same places where they are because you want to be in front of them. You want to see what they're seeing. You want them to see what you're talking about. You want to engage in their blogs, their websites, and social media. This is sort of a nice friendly stalking. You're not really stalking but you're being in their world and letting them know you're there. Initially you'll connect with them, maybe like them on Facebook or like them on Twitter, make a connection.

Then you'll start to like a little of their content, then make a few comments. You don't just come flying in like a crazy person. You come in casually and slowly, let them become aware of you and what you do. Once you have a connection and once they see you are respecting what they do. Then they might connect back.

As you engage with people, they will start to notice, especially if you do it constructively and with some responsibility. We are not trying to be a stalker, we are trying to contribute to the conversation. But you're going to contribute to the conversation with the people who are the key influencers and who later on might be people who are able to help you. When you come to release a new video or new product or a book or whatever it is you're going to do, these people will be there and will be in a position to help you. They will become invaluable because often if they are the top

Marketing Your Videos and You

influencers, they quite possibility have a very large network of people and connections. The key is to contribute to the conversation.

Moving Your Fans from Social Media to a Personal Connection?

Social media is one of the ways that you can build your platform. Ultimately what you want to have is an e-mail list of your fans. Social media sites like Facebook, Twitter, YouTube, etc., aren't necessarily selling platforms, though they can be, but it's a place to begin an engagement and connection.

From Social Media to a Personal Connection

Social Media **Engage**	Website **Following**	Email List **Connecting**
Facebook, Twitter Blab, Facebook Video Linkedin, YouTube	Use a Lead Magnet to Attract Subscribers Build an Email List	Books, Courses Videos, Content

You connect by liking or following someone, and hopefully they connect back. You start to build a small relationship. You engage with them. Then the goal is to move these fans from your social media pages to your website and then to your e-mail list. Most Internet marketing people regard the e-mail list as the most powerful form of connection to a person.

Connect to Your Audience with a Facebook Open Group

One of the places that I like a lot for connecting with people and building my platform is a Facebook Open Group. I have found it very powerful.

There are three kinds of Facebook groups; open groups, closed groups and secret groups. I'm talking here about an open group, which means people can see it in Facebook, people can search for it and see it, but they can't engage in it until they join it. People ask to join, the moderator (usually you) accepts them in and you have a connection.

I have a very popular Facebook Group called, 'How to Publish Your Book.' https://www.facebook.com/groups/HowToPublishYourBook/ We talk about publishing issues, ask questions, highlight new authors, and release books. Facebook groups are a very powerful way for me to build an audience.

Marketing Your Videos and You

Facebook open groups are focused around your topic not your name, so instead of it being the Bruce Jones group, it's How to Publish Your Book group. That's my topic. That's what I talk about. Use a group name that is focused on the subject. I engage with everyone, thank them for joining and make it personable.

The key for growing these groups is to engage people and share great content. I contribute content in the group on a regular basis. If I don't have anything original to write I'll find a good article, blog post, a video or something on a website that's good to share. Google Alerts are great for locating new content that I can share, it is not hard to do. https://www.google.com/alerts

I'm really the curator of content on my group and once it gets going, it kind of grows organically. People will ask and answer questions. It's also a great way to figure out what's going on in your market and what people are interested in. I keep everything focused and on the topic, I am the moderator. The goal is to keep your group focused on its topic, build a community and then eventually move fans over to your website to learn more about you and your content.

Every time I release content I promote it in my Facebook group. I think it's an incredibly valuable tool. Facebook is now all over the planet. It's the biggest and widest point of contact that everybody is familiar with, so check that out.

Connecting Live with Web Based Instant Personal Broadcasting
Another way to build an audience is to start using what I am calling instant personal broadcasting. These are apps and sites that allow you to conduct live video broadcasting with some kind of connection from the viewer back to the host. These connections can be live face to face, or just posted comments.

The major broadcasting applications right now are Blab.im, for desktop and mobile, Periscope, for smartphones, Google Hangout, for desktop and mobile and Facebook Video which is mostly mobile but also some desktop. Shortly to come is YouTube Connect and I am sure many more. If you Google any of these you can find out more information on them. All of these online platforms allow for very easy web-based connections with your

Marketing Your Videos and You

associates and anyone else. Where in the past it may have been very difficult to connect with someone to conduct a live, online interview, now it's getting easier and easier with platforms like Blab.

At the moment I am a big fan of Blab.im, it is so easy to use. It allows you to have up to four people talking at the same time. It has a social media built in. It has screen share, so you can run a webinar almost instantly. Great for interviews. And it records both the video and audio. Recording the content is becoming a key component of the instant personal broadcasting platforms. Type in your title, hit "broadcast" and you are live. These are great ways to get your message out there and to connect.

When done, load your broadcast up to YouTube, or take the audio file and create a podcast. You can now create content on the fly without anyone leaving your studio. The quality is excellent and the connection worldwide.

You're engaging with your audience very quickly and extremely cheaply. All of these broadcasting platforms are free. All you need is an Internet connection, a camera, mic, which is usually built into your computer, and you're ready to go. For many of them you can also embed the video code on your website and now you are broadcasting live from your own site, how cool is that. Easy to broadcast, easy to record and easy to connect with your audience and build a presence.

Facebook Live which now allows you to broadcast right into a Facebook Group or your personal page is coming on fast. Also don't forget about Google Hangout. This is a constantly changing space so pay attention.

Using YouTube to Build Your Community
Let's talk about YouTube. YouTube is for building a community. We often think of it as just the place where we host and share videos. But Google, which owns YouTube, also see it as a place to build community. Google sees it as a social media platform and it should be thought of in that manner. YouTube has likes, comments and subscriptions. I encourage you to think of YouTube as not just a place to promote your videos but a place that you can speak to your audience, break that video wall and connect with your viewer. Connections can be made by putting calls to action at the end of your videos to say "go do something, download something, visit some place."

Marketing Your Videos and You

Like Apple iTunes and podcasting, YouTube makes a huge effort to broadcast their video everywhere, so whether it's a phone, a desktop, a laptop, or anywhere that you can play a video, YouTube makes an effort to get it there. Their exposure is huge and worldwide.

Setting Up Your Videos on YouTube
There are three main areas to focus on when setting up your videos on YouTube. The first one is the title, then the description and then the social media connections. It is critical to have a descriptive title. You want to make sure your title is effective and it works from the first few words. You can put up to 100 characters in your title with 50 to 60 being ideal.

Setting Up Your YouTube Video • 3 Key Areas

Title, Up to 100 Characters, 50-60 is Good

A Well Written Description, With Up to 5,000 Characters and Live Web Links

A Live http Web Link

"In The Name of My Brother," by Sam Slosberg

Bill Gentile

631 views

Uploaded on Jun 9, 2011
http://videojournalismworkshops.com. WASHINGTON, DC, 9 June 2011 – In this powerful, deeply personal film, Sam Slosberg examines the struggle of one man whose brother, a Marine Corps sergeant, returned from Iraq with multiple ailments that eventually claimed his own life and forever changed the lives of his extended family. Sam was a participant in my 2-5 June 2011 Backpack Journalism Workshop in Washington, DC. A novice in this methodology and, until the workshop, untested in the technology that makes it possible, Sam nevertheless turned in a superior film on his first time out. My most sincere congratulations to him and to the other participants in our Backpack Journalism Workshop.

The second key area is your video description. Videos are found by Google and YouTube search and search works with words. Google and YouTube need to figure out what your video is about. Give it as many clues as you can. The very first thing in your video description, and this is key, is to put a live HTTP link for your website right at the beginning. HTTP is the entire web link. If you do that, your link will become a live link. You can send people back to your website or to someplace else. You can add about 5,000 characters to your description. You can have web links, transcript of the video text, social media connections, in there. You can really put a lot of information and really help YouTube figure out what your video is about.

Marketing Your Videos and You

YouTube is a Social Media Platform

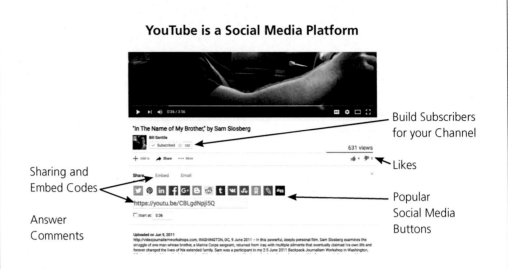

Build Subscribers for your Channel

Likes

Sharing and Embed Codes

Popular Social Media Buttons

Answer Comments

The third key area to help your videos get found is to use the social media tools that YouTube gives you. Everybody gets a channel on YouTube, that is your video home. If you have a Google account, you have a YouTube account. Ask people to subscribe to your channel. YouTube likes to see that. You have share buttons right below the video. Videos share very well on Facebook, Twitter, Linkedin and most of the other social media sites. You also have embed codes for sharing the video on your websites and blogs. This is a great way to spread your content and message.

Answer your YouTube comments. Every one. If you get comments on your videos, YouTube wants to see you answer it. They want to see you engaging. They don't want to see you put a video up, forget about it, and move on. You want to make sure that your videos are working for you and one of the ways is to answer the comments.

Your videos will get ranked and you will start to gain exposure if our engage with your audience. You will also learn a lot about what's going on with your videos by examining the stats in your YouTube Video Manager. Make sure the channel looks really good and has a good header graphic. Make sure you set up your profile and links. The more likes and subscribers you get, the higher YouTube will rank your video. Ask viewers to engage. Use the social media links below the video. Whenever I post a video on YouTube, I also embed it somewhere else and connect with all the social media I can. Video is a powerful tool for marketing and easy to spread. People love watching video. It's just enormously popular.

Marketing Your Videos and You

Marketing with Video

Make sure your videos are spread out over YouTube, Facebook, Google+, Linkedin, and more. Those are all powerful platforms and they all reach different audiences in different ways. Don't forget your own website.

You just don't want to be in one spot. Be in as many places as you can and get your message and your videos and your content spread around. Social media is just one aspect. You can do little snippets of video on Instagram which is becoming immensely popular. Snapchat's becoming popular. Wherever your audience is, you need to be. Remember at the beginning we talked about being where your audience is. Figure that out and then make sure that your content is in all of those places and is properly described, with good titles, all the correct links. Be sure everything is working.

I encourage everybody to have their own website or a blog. Some kind of web-based home. Some place where you center all your content. I want to talk about that in just a moment but basically you want to be in some place where everything you do can be focused and then you can reach out from and connect with all of your content.

Along with live personal broadcasting we also have platforms like Google Hangout, Zoom.us and Skype.com. These are very popular sites for broadcasting to small audiences and can be added into your mix for connecting. What is great about these tools is that they all have a global reach for almost no cost. They are easy ways to take your content and expand it and extend it.

Cross connect everything. Whatever platforms you're on, make sure that you connect all the other platforms. If you're on Facebook, link people over to Twitter, on Twitter to your website.

Marketing Your Video by Building a Website or Blog

I think everybody should have some kind of web platform. It can be a blog or a website but somewhere you focus all of your content and information. If your site is not a blog be sure to have a blogging page so that you're building a continual presence online. Be sure to cross connect all of your social media and web properties. People need to be able to interact with you and your content on different platforms. Google loves this, and your audience loves this.

Marketing Your Videos and You

Think of an idea like a wagon wheel, you're bringing everybody in to a central place from around the web to learn about you, your content and then hopefully connect so that you can continue the conversation, sell them something, get an assignment or build your presence.

One of the key pages on this site is an About page. It's one of the highest visited pages on any blog page or website. It's kind of like your LinkedIn page but it's also on your website.

Along with your About page, you also want to have a Media page. If someone is going to interview or promote you then this is where they go to get the facts. You might have a several bios of different lengths, headshots with different poses. You should have access to your videos with descriptions and or a video trailer. Links to other interviews, and other relevant content.

Every website should have an e-mail sign up box. You need to be gathering the e-mail address of your fans. Two of the more popular sites for managing e-mail are MailChimp and Aweber but there are many, many other companies. Here's where we talked about having a lead magnet, so somewhere on your site you want to move people to sign up for your e-mail list and give away something, maybe it's a little behind-the-scenes video that you don't have anywhere else. Maybe it's a little guide book on your topic. Doesn't have to be big or take a long time to make. Just something you have done, something you know about that your audience might be interested in, and you can use that as a friendly thank you for people to come.

Then super important is a way to buy your products or services. We can't just do all these things for free, so you have a products page or a store page or something like that. These are your DVDs or maybe your streaming video or whatever it is that you're doing, maybe a course you've put together, but you need some way that people can interact with you and buy your stuff. Marketing your videos and you is a key component of your website.

Being Consistent with Your Marketing

You can't just put up a website and be done with it. You have to interact with your site and audience on a regular basis. You need to build some consistency with your audience interaction. If you're going to release a bunch of new content, maybe instead of all at once, release it once a week

Marketing Your Videos and You

over a period of weeks so that Google and your audience sees continually new content. You don't have to make a video every week. You might release a blog post this week. You might release a little news item the next. This also gives you something to promote and can be very effective to building audience.

Along with releasing good content on a regular basis, be sure all your contact info and bios are current and up-to-date, across all your platforms. Not just on your website, but anywhere you are, including Facebook, in LinkedIn. This information just goes out of date really quickly and we forget we even have it, so it's a key part of keeping things up-to-date.

We also don't just have to be online. We kind of forget that there's a whole offline world. Check with your local media. You have newspapers and organizations that have a local presence. Go out to the market, give a talk, maybe make a meet-up group. Local media loves to hear what you're doing. They're always looking for content, especially the local paper. It's a great way to get that out there. It's all about making connections in all the different ways we can and linking everybody together.

Selling Your Work to the World

When you're making content, you always want to be thinking about how you are going to sell it. You might be making content for a non-profit organization or you're doing a film on a current topic but you always want to be thinking about, "How can I sell this? What else can I do with this content? Can I repurpose this and make other products from it?"

If you are able to sell your video content you want to make sure that your content is clean and that you own all the rights to it. You need to have all the signed releases including people, locations and materials. Do you have the rights to the logos, music, and trademarks, so that you can sell it and use it as you want? Usually we don't want to have trademark logos or any unlicensed music in the backgrounds. If you are going to repurpose your content then shoot your footage free and clear. If you're just doing news, then the logos and trademarks and things may just kind of go along but if you're going to use this content later on, you want it to be as clean as you possibly can.

Marketing Your Videos and You

The other thing I recommend for you to do when you're creating video content is to bring a still camera of some kind with you. It can be your smartphone or it could be another camera. There are tons to choose from. The key is to put the video camera down and take stills of what you're shooting. Having those stills can be extremely helpful when you get to editing. They can really save you if you have missed something. But also very useful when you're marketing and selling your work.

Think Editorially as You Create Your Content
You may be shooting a single story and your audience may be seeing a single story but in your head you should be thinking editorially about how you could combine several stories together to make a longer show or some other kind of products. If you are thinking editorially you can craft a plan over a period of time and block out other stories and products.

I encourage you to think bigger. Think editorially. Think broader than just a single piece of work. It's part of a connected stream of work that you can use to do a lot more with. The individual becomes a series. Now, and this is key, series don't have to be 28 minutes or an hour long for a network. Series can be three minutes long for 20 videos that you put on YouTube. YouTube is a powerful distribution platform for many, many series and the series can be very short, so you don't have to go crazy trying to make these things.

Seed Your Work for Later Sales
Think about the work and what it can be. If you're doing a longer piece, can it be cut up into little pieces and turned into multiple videos? That's thinking editorially. You can create multiple pieces of content all from one single effort. Having a companion book that goes along with your video can be a powerful way to get some extra income.

For marketing have your web address appear along the bottom of the videos. A lot of people don't watch the entire video, they only watch the first 20 to 30 seconds. Even though we'd love them to watch the whole thing, make sure you have a call to action right up at the front. It can be subtle. You could have just your name and maybe a web address right below. Also include a closing screen where viewers can go to get more info or follow up products. Give viewers a way to continue the story and the connection.

Marketing Your Videos and You

Act Local, Think Global

YouTube and Facebook and the web, are all global platforms. You may be shooting a story for just your market, just your town, community, or organization, but in reality that video is being seen around the world. You want to think that way, like, "Is this working in other countries and if I have a call to action for a book or some kind of a companion PDF that goes with my piece, can people from Europe download my piece? Can they get that?"

You want to think globally, it's a big world, there's a huge audience out there, so act local but think global with your content.

Distributing and Selling Your Content Worldwide

We have worldwide access now to distribute, market, broadcast and deliver our content. The gatekeepers have fallen. We have access now to distribute our content everywhere in the world using platforms like Vimeo, YouTube and Facebook. YouTube is probably the dominating one but Facebook is becoming huge in the power of distributing content and the power of free.

You can send your content everywhere so you want to make sure it's in all the places that it can be. Vimeo has Vimeo Pro on Demand, so you can earn some money from it. There are also many other ways of selling it, VHX, Apple iTunes, podcast. These are all just ways of distributing content. The days of stock photo and selling aren't as big and rich as they used to be but they're still there and sites like Shutterstock, Getty, iStockPhoto and many more are constantly looking for stills and video footage. If you're going to do stock footage and photos, be sure to read the rules. Take some of that extra footage that you have and put it up and sell it on some of these sites.

Sell Your Own Shows and Stories

There is no reason you can't sell your own content on your own site. You have worked hard to develop these films. Showcase them. With video on demand there are a lot of sites now that you can use as a host and sell your own content. That's a pretty cool way to do things and using different back office technologies like Gumroad, Teachable and Vimeo Pro you can broadcast and sell your own stories. At your finger tips you have all the hosting, streaming, marketing and advertising platforms you will need.

One of the sites that I have used a lot and I love it for doing things like this, is a site called Gumroad.com. Gumroad.com is sort of an electronic bucket

Marketing Your Videos and You

where you can upload all kinds of content. It can be video content, audio, PDFs, zip files, anything really that you can get up online you can put here and they give you the ability to sell and distribute it. It is a self-contained little e-commerce platform.

Sites like this give you the ability to host your content, sell it, accept payments and then distribute the content to your fans with streaming or download. They also handle all the e-commerce back-office stuff and put the money in your bank account. They really cater to content creators, to storytellers, especially in the video area. If you want to have a platform for selling your content, this is a great way to go. The costs are very, very low. Start selling your stories right on your own website.

Amazon Video Direct

This is brand new and we don't know quite exactly where this is going yet but Amazon has now opened up their Amazon Prime site and released Amazon Video Direct. https://videodirect.amazon.com/

It's a little more complicated than Gumroad. There are a few more hoops you have to go through including a little more complicated upload process. But you're on Amazon and it's a great way to sell your content and reach a huge world. Amazon is enormously respected and trusted by everybody so I would take a serious look at this. This is coming out now and they are looking for content creators and storytellers with movie shorts, TV show and web series.

Like YouTube, Amazon also makes a huge effort to spread their content and make sure that people can actually see it and view it. On royalties, that's what it's all about, making money off of our content and Amazon is a fantastic platform to be on. I have used the print side of Amazon, CreateSpace, for years for my book content and now we have access for videos so check that out. Just search on Amazon Video Direct and you'll get to it.

Products from Videos, Re-purposing Your Content

You've gone through all the work to make that video story, so what else can you do with it? Some people like video products, some people like to read, some people like audio, you can release all formats. You can strip your videos down and pull out the audio track and sell that. You can transcribe

Marketing Your Videos and You

your videos and use the text to create a lot of other products like books and manuals. Maybe you did an interview as part of your story and maybe you only used a small part of it. Why not transcribe the entire interview and turn it into a book that you can sell as a companion piece or a standalone product? From your video you can create physical books and Kindle e-book, blog posts, manuals and courses. How about building a talk or a course or just more in-depth content? Remember all those stills we grabbed with the second camera, they make for a great travel book, or illustrated guide.

For transcribing your video or audio content look at sites like Rev.com, great site to work with. Rev.com will transcribe your video for about a dollar a minute.

You can do an interview with someone on video, that video can go on iTunes as a video podcast. Pull out the audio and you have an audio podcast. You can also sell that audio or video stream, remember Gumroad.com. You can put the video on YouTube as just a video, so you're getting a lot of different uses out of doing something one time. You can use it to do webinars, Google Hangouts, YouTube, live streaming. These are all things that you can build out of making your video. I'm really encouraging you to look at this. It's not just doing a video but doing a whole series of things that you can use and sort of relate and intersect together. Think editorially.

Speaking of opportunities, especially if you're doing video, you are speaking to the world so why not say, "Hey, I can come and speak to your organization on this same topic." You see journalists all the time doing it on news programs. Take your texts and your videos and push them out there.

Don't forget educational online learning. If you are traveling to fun places you can easily shoot extra content, or stay an extra day. Finish the story and shoot the travel video.

Look at Rick Steves and his PBS travel videos, travel stories are big. He's going out and making basically short documentaries of all the different places he visits and he turns around and they become educational material. You can take what you're learning in one place and turn it into something else. One of the biggest educational sites is Udemy.com, rearrange your story and teach a course on your topic. Teachable is a course site that is pretty easy to use. I mentioned Gumroad already. There are many great places to build courses around your content.

Marketing Your Videos and You

You can take the images and videos that you have and make stock video imagery out of it. You just want to read the rules that Shutter Stock and Getty and others have, but if you don't have logos in the background and your footage isn't shaky, you can cut it up into little pieces and send it off as stock.

One of the major places to distribute content is Amazon and there's a number of different ways to do it. We already talked about Amazon Instant Video streaming. You've made a documentary or a news piece, maybe take two or three or four of those, string them together, you have now an instant show, put it on Amazon Instant Video. You can also use Createspace, Createspace is Amazon's print on demand side and you can transcribe your video and make books out of it. CreateSpace also has a DVD side so if you'd like to distribute DVD content, Createspace.com is a place to take a look at for doing that. Print-on-demand is a powerful idea for keeping your content under cost control.

Take the same text you just made the print book from and you can go into Kindle with an e-book. It's a great platform. Everything in Kindle is the e-platform side of Amazon. It can be just text or text and pictures, or just pictures. Remember all those stills. Amazon is accepted everywhere. Everybody loves it. It's a great place to be. You can take content that you're creating and spread it around the world. Amazon isn't the only platform, there are lots of other book platforms you can work with.

One of the big advantages of self-publishing is that you don't lose control of your rights over your content. On Amazon and other sites you retain all rights, it is non-exclusive. Which means you can distribute how you want. CreateSpace and Kindle are non-exclusive sites so you can take the same content, format it, and put it out through Nook which is the Barnes and Noble e-book platform or Kobo another global platform for e-books. We also have print on demand product sites like Zazzle.com, Cafepress.com and more to make calendars, mugs, pillow, clocks, etc. It goes on and on.

There are lots of ways to get your content out there. Remember one thing that's happening a lot with Kindle books and regular books is that you can put live links in a Kindle book. You can put up a Kindle book about your trip to the Congo and put live links in the text that can send people to your website or to YouTube or to maybe a page where they can buy the whole

Marketing Your Videos and You

series. You can cross between these different platforms.

That's a very, very simple thing to do, to put a live link in a Kindle book and send people to go get the whole series. You can do a book of your adventures in the Congo and what you're doing and then send them off to a site where they can buy the video packages that go with that book. A very, very powerful way of using all the technologies together to create content and profit.

If you're looking at books for the bookstore market then look at IngramSpark. CreateSpace and Kindle are primarily just Amazon and they just stay on Amazon. IngramSpark is the world's largest book distributor with 39,000 stores and partners to work with. They primarily use print-on-demand and they distribute books around the planet. If you see bookstores as part of your mix, IngramSpark might be a place to look.

I'm J. Bruce Jones. I hope you enjoyed this chapter on launching your content and yourself to the world and making some money from it. I encourage you to make content, sell it and distribute to the world.

You can reach me on Facebook, Twitter and at my blog.
https://www.facebook.com/groups/HowToPublishYourBook/ • @bjdesign
http://brucethebookguy.blogspot.com/ • 781-492-0742

Bill Gentile

Washington, DC
Cell: (202) 492-6405
Web sites: www.billgentile.com, http://billgentile.com/live-workshops
E-mail: billgentile@billgentile.com
Twitter: @billgentile

I am an independent journalist and documentary filmmaker teaching at American University in Washington, DC. My career spans four decades, five continents and nearly every facet of journalism and mass communication, most especially visual communication, or visual storytelling. I am the founder and director of American University's Backpack Journalism Project. I am a pioneer of "backpack video journalism" and today am one of the craft's most noted practitioners. I authored the highly acclaimed "Essential Video Journalism Field Manual." I engineered the School of Communication's 2015-2017 partnership with the Pulitzer Center on Crisis Reporting and am the driving force behind that initiative.

Photo by Carlos Ernesto Escalona

My recent work includes "When the Forest Weeps," a short film that examines how Ecuador's Kichwa Indians struggle as their deep spiritual relationship with the Amazonian rain forest diminishes in a clash with the forces of so-called modernity. (See https://www.youtube.com/watch?v=Wgqh6PGw1lg)

My work also includes the 2015 documentary, "Afghan Dreams," which I shot, produced and wrote, about four Afghan law students – all female – who defy all odds to compete in the world's most important competition of international commercial law. In 2013, I shot, produced, wrote and narrated a three-part film series on religion and gangs in Guatemala. The three films, "I. The Gangs," "II. The Researcher," and "III. The Pastor," are viewable on YouTube at http://www.youtube.com/watch?v=Eu2gRjMyacc, at http://www.youtube.com/watch?v=E3wnOfHQemY, and at http://www.youtube.com/watch?v=Bl7fZnPQjR0, respectively.

My one-hour documentary, "Through Their Eyes," was released in 2013. Shot during a four-month teaching assignment in Cuba, the film follows six American University students studying there during fall semester 2011. "Through Their Eyes" explores Cuba, off-limits to most Americans since the 1960s, through the eyes of these young Americans. And it documents the students' profound transformation during their stay on that forbidden island.

Additional work in Cuba includes "Reading While They Roll: Cuba's Cigar Factory Tradition," for Time.com at http://www.time.com/time/video/player/0,32068,1465077893001_2108125,00.html. Also on the Time Magazine Web site, see "Cuba's (Rocky) Love Affair with the Harley-Davidson" at http://www.time.com/time/video/player/0,32068,1535177462001_2111035,00.html.

My story for USA Today on the Cuban economy can be seen at http://www.usatoday.com/news/world/story/2012-06-07/cuba-economy-castro/55448580/1

My previous works include "Nurses Needed," about the nursing shortage across the United States, and "Afghanistan: The Forgotten War," about America's deepening involvement in that Central Asian country. Broadcast in 2008 by NOW on PBS, the stories were named NOW's Number 1 and Number 3, respectively, most popular of the year. For the Afghanistan piece, I was a finalist for a national Emmy Award.

I worked as Documentary Consultant on "The White House: Inside America's Most Famous Home." This full-length documentary was the centerpiece of C-SPAN's weeklong programming about the presidents' home. The documentary, for which C-SPAN gained unprecedented access to areas of the White House never before filmed, aired nationwide on 14 November 2008, and has aired numerous times since then. The DVD of the documentary has become the best-selling DVD ever distributed by C-SPAN.

In July-August 2013, I traveled to St. Petersburg, Russia, and participated as a delegate in the 4th meeting of the U.S.-Russia Bilateral Presidential Commission (BPC) Sub-Group on Mass Media. The commission is the premier forum between the U.S. and Russia to strengthen relations with each respective government and society. President Obama and President Medvedev established the BPC in July 2009 to reset U.S.-Russia relations and to engage the Russian government to pursue foreign policy goals of common interest for the American and Russian people.

I began in 1977 as reporter for the Mexico City News and correspondent for United Press International (UPI) based in Mexico City. I covered the 1979 Sandinista Revolution in Nicaragua. I spent two years as editor on UPI's Foreign Desk in New York, then moved to Nicaragua and became Newsweek Magazine's Contract Photographer for Latin America and the Caribbean. My book of photographs, "Nicaragua," won the Overseas Press Club Award for Excellence. I covered the U.S.-backed Contra War in Nicaragua and the Salvadoran Civil War in the 1980s; the U.S. invasion of

Panama; the 1994 invasion of Haiti, the ongoing conflict with Cuba, the 1990-91 Persian Gulf War and the subsequent wars in Iraq and Afghanistan. I've also worked in Ivory Coast, Guinea, Sierra Leone, Chad, Angola, Rwanda and Burundi.

In 1995 I went to work for Video News International (VNI), precursor of The New York Times Television Company. I completed assignments for The Learning Channel, the Discovery Channel, National Geographic Television, ABC's Nightline With Ted Koppel, NOW With Bill Moyers, NOW hosted by David Brancaccio, Court TV and Lion TV.

I shared the Robert F. Kennedy Award for Human Rights Reporting, Honorable Mention, for a story on rape during the 1994 Rwanda Genocide. I shared two National Emmy Awards and was nominated for two others.

My documentary, "DATELINE AFGHANISTAN: Reporting the Forgotten War," about foreign correspondence in Afghanistan, premiered in March 2006. The film competed as official entry to the 15th Annual Woods Hole Film Festival. It competed in the 2007 Washington DC Independent Film Festival.

I am a Journalist-in-Residence at American University, where I created that institution's Foreign Correspondence Network (FCN). I am featured in two award-winning documentaries about international journalism in Nicaragua, "The World Is Watching" and a sequel, "The World Stopped Watching."

My Video Journalism Workshops, http://billgentile.com/live-workshops, have received wide acclaim. I have conducted video workshops and presentations in the United States, Mexico, Guatemala, Nicaragua, El Salvador, Panama, Uruguay, Venezuela, Suriname, Thailand, Ghana, Cuba and the former Soviet Republic of Georgia, for the U.S. Department of State, the Thomson Reuters Foundation, the Thai Broadcast Journalist Association, American University's Center for Latin American and Latino Studies (CLALS), and others.

I am featured in a video produced by the State Department to promote "citizen journalism" around the world. The video is titled, "Raise Your Voice."

https://www.youtube.com/watch?v=HIDnpVMzlBc

I received an undergraduate degree at Penn State University. I acquired a Master's Degree at Ohio University in Athens, Ohio. I am fluent in Spanish and have conducted numerous workshops and presentations in Spanish.

VI.
Epilogue

Congratulations on having arrived at the end of my Essential Video Journalism Field Manual. But this is just the end of the beginning. You now are equipped with a body of knowledge that, as in my case, can serve as a ticket and a tool, helping to introduce you to people and places that you otherwise might not get to know or to visit. Moreover, this knowledge can serve as your tool in allowing you to take part in the global exchange of ideas and information, and to impact change in the world. So use this knowledge wisely. Use it judiciously. Use it with love.

Good luck. Stay safe. And keep in touch.

Bill Gentile
Summer 2016

Made in the USA
San Bernardino, CA
11 November 2016